NICK SAN

MW01152517

VICTIM TO VICTOR

BY

NICK SANTONASTASSO

1

VICTIM TO VICTOR

Ordering Information:

Quantity sales. Special discounts are available on quantity purchases by corporations, associations, and others.

Orders by U.S. trade bookstores and wholesalers. Please contact NICK @ www.BookNickSanto.com

Edited and Marketed By

DreamStarters University

www.DreamStartersUniversity.com

Foreword by Ed Mylett

*"Nick exemplifies the **Maxing Out Life** to the fullest!*

His story is truly special and inspirational.

I would go anywhere in the world to hear him speak."

Ed Mylett

Top 50 Wealthiest Under 50, Host of #MAXOUT Podcast

Testimonials

"First time I heard Nick story, was on YouTube, i started watching that same video daily cause it really helped me cutting all the excuses out of my daily, now I'm humbled and honored to call him a friend and a great inspiration, he is a force of Nature, truly a statement in defying the odds and one of the greatest speakers I have had the pleasure to work with."
— Fabio Viviani, Celebrity Chef, Hospitality Developer and Restaurateur, NYT Best Selling Author

Nick has every excuse to play the victim card in his life but he doesn't. He has accepted the cards he has been dealt and used his circumstances in life to inspire the masses. I have met many inspiring people in my life and Nick ranks up there with the best!
— Rob Dial - Speaker, Coach and host of The Mindset & Motivation Podcast

One of my favorite humans in the world because he gets it. Nick exudes the mind set that we all need to be on. He sees life without the imaginary "i cant" attitude. He lives in reality where he isn't held back by the imaginary wall of self-limiting beliefs we hide behind.
— Michie Peachie
Model, Fitness entrepreneur

"One of the rules I live my life by is, no matter what happens in life, good and bad, as long as your alive, it's still your mutha fuckin set!, Nick Santonastaasso is the physical and mental embodiment of this mantra"
— CT Fletcher Fitness Legend

Nick became my mentor way before I heard him speak. Seeing him do things and goin places inspired me to think big

and believe in myself. He is one of the most influential and motivating speakers of our generation, no doubt.
— Artemus Dolgin, athlete, designer and CEO of Golden Aesthetics, INC.

"I've got to know Nick thru the sport of wrestling when he came and spoke to the kids in my club. This was the early days of his speaking career and right from the start you could tell this is what he was destined for. It's amazing to see his career flourish in such a short time. Nick Santonastasso is an inspiration to us all."
— Frankie Edgar Former UFC Lightweight Champion.

"I heard Nick speak for the first time at our GoBundance mastermind in Austin, Texas. Nick captivated, inspired and shifted the perspectives of about 60 successful business men. Afterwards he auctioned one free speech and that's where I locked him down for my companies."
— David Osborn New York Times best-selling author of Wealth Can't Wait.

"My daughter has arthrogryposis and underwent amputations last spring. I use your page for inspiration for her and also with my patients. It does make a difference-- Especially with the preteen boys. Thanks for all that you do."
— Liz Storholt

"Hi, I'm Eri from Japan. I am currently studying at the college in the US and I just wanted to thank you for encouraging me to keep trying things, I am so lucky to find your video on Instagram. Thank you for showing us your BEAUTY."
— Eri Watanabe

"Thank you Nick! This was a great episode and your story is very inspirational. I love your message of taking action steps opposed to living with a victim mentality."
— Laura Olsen

"This is my fourth year going to GYLS [Tony Robbins youth leadership] and honestly I have never had someone influence me as much as you did. Thank you for your kindness, courage and authenticity that is so refreshing in this crazy world. Come back to Jersey, we'd love to have you."
— Ireland Horan

"Hi Nick. I heard your interview with Ed Mylett and I just wanted to let you know how much it impacted me. You have a real gift for speaking and you completely took my excuses away (thank you for that). You are really wise beyond your years, and I hope that one day I grow to the point of having that incredible mindset that you do."
— Marissa John

"Nick!!! You have literally just changed my life bro and I appreciate you for being exactly who you are and your incredible perspective!! I have not felt emotions like I did listening to you in long time."
— Jesse Schmitz

"Wow Nick, incredible podcast interview with the incredible Ed Mylett. You dropped so many nuggets.
"Adaptation", forget the outside noise, learning to pull the good from every situation, we are the architect of our own life. Need to force ourselves to level up, if not ready, just jump in! Just a few things that I took from it. Thank you so much."
— Art Villanueva

Table of Contents

Chapter 1

From Victim to Victor

"Two men looked out from prison bars. One saw the mud, the other saw the stars"
Dale Carnegie

This book is designed to get you to view your world in a new way. Sometimes it takes a different person, from a different walk of life, who's been through different challenges, to break through the barrier of your perspective. Within these pages, I'm going share with you my life, the challenges I've faced and how I overcame them. This book is meant to help people from all walks of life—entrepreneurs, salespeople, CEOs, teachers, stay-at -home moms, high school students, college students and everyone in between.

I did not write this book just to talk about myself. I wrote it so you, too, can experience a shift in your life towards greater fulfillment and a greater sense of gratitude. Even if you've already heard everything I'm about to say, my hope is that what I'm going to share will resonate with you in a new way and inspire you to live your life to the fullest.

Take a moment right now to thank yourself for picking up this book and actually opening it up to read it. The fact that you are willing to invest in yourself by reading this book tells me that you are ready to take your life to the next level. You are ready to stop living life as a **VICTIM**, and you're ready to become the **VICTOR** of your life's story. You are no longer willing to settle for how life has always been. You are ready to actively create the future, the life you have always wanted!

We all need reminders now and then of what is important in life. We all need someone to shake up our daily routine and show us that life is vibrant and alive. Think of it like this. When you're a student going to school, and your parents or teachers tell you to do your homework, you may not want to listen. It may feel like your parents or teachers are always nagging you to do something. Your attitude might be, "Why should I listen?"

That is, until you meet someone you really look up to, maybe a professional athlete, actor or musical artist, and they tell you that doing your homework is important. Suddenly, doing your homework becomes a priority. Your perspective has totally shifted.

When you relate with someone differently and they give you good advice, it can powerfully shift the way you look at your life. This is why I want you to get to know me. I want you to be able to relate to me on a personal level.

Maybe what I share with you in this book will help you break the barrier of your perspective and eliminate limiting beliefs you may have about your life. What you will learn in this book can change you, if you're willing to let it. I know because I myself have changed as I've learned through experience what I'm going to share with you.

It doesn't matter who you are or what advantages or disadvantages you were born with. If you're willing to learn and apply the lessons in this book, you can take your life to a level of peak performance you've never reached before. Here are some of the most profound benefits you can expect to gain when you read and apply what you will learn in this book. You will:

- Turn your "losses and failures" into gifts
- Gain more confidence in all areas of your life
- Be present and enjoy the time that you have with the people you love the most
- Experience more gratitude and less worry
- Uncover and begin living your life's purpose
- Stop settling for less than you can be, share or do and start living in alignment

I realize I'm making a lot of bold claims here, and this might come across as overpromising. It might sound a little too good to be true. But I can assure you there is no hyperbole here. This book is going to show you how to become the person you need to be and improve every area of your life.

The first step in the whole process is changing the way you look at the world. What lens are you currently looking at the world through? Is it the lens of the **VICTIM**, or is it the lens of the **VICTOR**? Be honest with yourself and answer this question on the line below:

_____

No matter your answer right now, you can become the VICTOR! Now, when you examine your core values, how do they hold up? Are they serving you? What do you think is stopping you from living the life you really want to live? What challenges are you facing?

How you view the world is a habit, and if you view it negatively right now, it's going to require discipline to change that. It's going to require you to obtain victory over what you currently think of as "you." You're going to have to defeat your mind.

Your biggest enemy is not the government. Your biggest enemy is not the way you were raised. Your biggest enemy is not your friends or your boss. Your biggest enemy is you and your mindset.

In life, when you begin to understand this, something profound happens. You begin to reclaim power that you didn't even know you had inside of you. You begin to realize the greatest disadvantage you can ever have is a bad mindset, and that you are the only person responsible for your mindset.

Nobody else is responsible for what goes on inside of your head on a daily basis except for you. Now, most people hinder their success simply because of the way they think. If you can change the way you think, you can change your entire life.

I speak to a lot of different people on a regular basis when I give talks at schools, conventions, corporations, churches, etc. What I've discovered is that people from all walks of life, all of whom have achieved varying degrees of "success" in the world, all suffer from the same types of internal problems.

It's not just young people that struggle with anxiety, depression and feelings of not knowing their place in the world. There is no point in life or magic number in your bank account where all of your problems just melt away. You have to make a conscious choice to change the way you're going to view the world, or you may suffer the consequences of having a negative mindset for your entire life.

At a recent event I spoke at, a 60 year old gentleman came up to me with his eyes full of tears after I was done speaking, and he told me, "Because of you, I will never think the same way again. I will never look at the world the way I have for my entire life up to now." The day this man had heard me speak started off all wrong. The tire pressure light in his car turned on when he got in the car. He then got stuck in traffic, and his entire day was ruined by these two minor annoyances.

After hearing my story and what I've done to overcome some extreme challenges in my life, this gentleman made a decision after 60 years of living one way, to completely change his mindset. He flipped a switch, and he decided he did not want to look at the world as he had for decades.

The tire pressure being low in your car or being caught in traffic might not seem like big reasons to get upset. Shockingly, many people allow small things like this to totally derail their days on a regular basis. We are primed to focus on our problems and our disadvantages our whole lives, and this creates negative emotional patterns that turn into negative mindsets that we can't help but get trapped in.

This is why it's so important for you to realize that you can think differently. You can change the meaning that you attach to the things that you experience in life. This is the incredible strength that we all have as human beings. You can pull the good from everything. By picking up this book, you've already taken a huge first step towards changing the way you experience your life. Together, we are about to embark on the journey from **Victim to Victor**.

As you go through this book, keep a pen, pencil or highlighter handy. When you come across something that stands out to you, circle it, highlight it and make a quick note of why you think it's important or anything else that it brings to mind. This book is your tool for personal growth! Don't worry about marking it up, because for you to really learn and grow from what's taught here, you have to engage with the content on a personal level. You want to walk away from this book with lessons you can apply to your life, not just having read a nice story. So, be hands on, and get ready to make this book—and your life—your own!

Chapter Summary

Your perspective in life is extremely powerful. It guides you and influences how you feel and the choices that you make. Sometimes it takes a different person who has gone through different experiences and overcome different challenges in life to pierce through the barrier of your perspective and get you to see the world in a new way. That's the purpose of this book.

Many people go through life with the same negative mindset for their whole lives. There is no point in life that a negative mindset goes away on its own, unless you decide to do something about it. Even older people, like a 60 year old man I met at an event I spoke at recently, struggle with reacting negatively to everything that happens to them. This is because people are primed throughout their life to respond in a negative way when something they consider bad happens to them.

But you, as a human being, have the power to change the meaning you attach to everything you experience in life. You can pull good from any situation. Your biggest enemy is not outside of you. Your biggest enemy is yourself and your negative mindset. By picking up this book, you've already taken a huge step towards changing the way you view and experience life. We are about to embark on the journey from **Victim to Victor**.

Questions to Answer Before You Continue Reading...

- Why are you here, reading this book?
- What is important to you?
-
- What does success look like for you?

_____

_____

_____

_____

_____

_____

_____

_____

_____

_____

_____

_____

_____

_____

_____

_____

"The only limits you have are the ones you put on yourself"

Nick Santonastasso

Chapter 2

Start Your Day With Gratitude

"Gratitude makes sense of our past, brings peace for today, and creates a vision for tomorrow"

Melody Beattie

My parents had three children before they had me and late in the pregnancy my parents went for an ultrasound. Everything was going great, and they were looking forward to taking a look at their baby.

The doctor used ultrasound equipment to pull up an image of me on a large screen. Several doctors in the room began to look at each other with puzzled expressions on their faces. My parents asked them, "Is there something wrong? Is there a problem?"

The response was far from what they expected, "Well, Mr. and Mrs. Santonastasso, the results of the ultrasound show there are no legs, we can only detect one arm, and we

18

can't see the other. There also may be defects to the organs and a possible cleft palate."

Right there, in the doctor's office, my parents promised each other they were going to raise this child just like their other three, and see where life takes this.

When I was born, I was diagnosed with Hanhart syndrome. Hanhart syndrome is a rare genetic disorder that either leaves babies with undeveloped limbs or undeveloped organs. I was the 12th baby in medical history to receive this diagnosis.

Out of 12 babies, 8 had passed away due to undeveloped organs. Some babies with Hanhart syndrome may need life support equipment to keep their organs functioning and may need feeding tubes.

My parents were also told that I had about a 30% chance to live. In spite of this, they kept moving forward with the pregnancy, and my mom gave birth to me by way of C-section.

As soon as I was born, my parents immediately focused on the good in the situation. My mom has told me that the first thing she noticed when she saw me for the first time was that I was beautiful, and had a full head of hair. Doctors performed tests on my organs, and all of them came back 100% healthy.

When I think back on this, how I had a 30% chance to live, how only 12 babies in medical history had been diagnosed with this condition at the time, all I can think about is how rare it is for me to be here, alive, in this very moment. When I think about this, it's a reminder to be super grateful about the simple fact that I'm alive.

Life itself, just being here, is a miracle. You, yourself, as a human being, are a rare, improbable phenomenon, just because you're alive. Do you know how many sperm died trying to bring you to life? The odds of you coming into existence were slim to none, and yet you are here.

This is why every single human being, including you, has a reason to be grateful. Living in this state of gratitude is so important because **it is emotionally impossible for you to feel grateful and sad at the same time. It's also emotionally impossible for you to feel grateful and angry at the same time**.

The emotion of gratitude outweighs all negative emotions. This is scientifically proven, but daily life can get hectic and busy and it's easy to forget to be grateful. This is why when I wake up I always start my day by thinking of five things I'm grateful for. I have my tribe do this, too.

We all think about five things we're grateful for and write them down. This is how you start your day off on the right foot. I don't even have a foot, and I can still start my day off on the right one, so you can too. No matter who you are.

When you start your day with gratitude, you receive a morale boost. You receive the right energy to use going into your day with intention and purpose. As you continually write down the reasons you're grateful each morning, your mind gets into the rhythm. To help you learn more and experience the feeling of gratitude on a deeper level, I created a Virtual Training course where I do a deep dive into practicing gratitude in daily life. (You can find more info on this course at *booknicksanto.com*.)

I call writing down the things you're grateful for every morning creating a "gratitude journal." When you first start creating a gratitude journal, you might write down big things you're thankful for, like your house, your family and your job. As you keep up with it, you will start to notice all the things you would normally take for granted and what a blessing they really are.

You'll begin to write reasons such as, "I have clothes on my back, my refrigerator is full, and I have air conditioning to keep me cool in the heat. Also, I have hot water that comes out of my shower every time I turn it on and water to drink that's cold." There is truly an abundance of reasons to be grateful that go unnoticed by most people on a daily basis.

Even hardships are experiences you can be grateful for. When you remember good things that have happened, it's easy to see the big picture. What if you looked at the struggles you have had in life you thought were negative, and they actually turned out to be defining and important for you?

Tragic things happen to everyone, but you can choose to face these differently. You don't have to pretend that your struggles aren't challenging, but if you can see the good in them, your thoughts in your daily life will transform.

You can even be grateful for your future. Picture the best possible future for yourself.

Focusing on this future will provide you with a sense of direction.

None of us can 100% control the circumstances we find ourselves in throughout life, good or bad, but we can always choose to be grateful. You might find yourself overwhelmed by negative feelings on a daily basis, but I want to challenge you to develop gratitude whenever this happens. I think you will be surprised to find that this will totally erase your negative thoughts if you give it enough practice. **So start every day by thinking about and writing down five things you're grateful for.**

I want to challenge you for the next 30 days to post five things you're grateful for (that's how long it takes to form a habit) in our online community on Facebook.

For more information on the Victorious community please visit www.booknicksanto.com

Chapter Summary

I was the fourth child to be born into my family. When my parents went in for a late in the pregnancy ultra-sound, they were told that my limbs were not developing. I didn't have one of my arms, and I didn't have any legs. Right there, in that moment, my parents determined they were going to raise me just like they raised their other children. They decided they were going to see where life took them.

After birth, I was diagnosed with a rare genetic condition called Hanhart syndrome. Before me, only 12 other babies in medical history had ever been diagnosed with this before me at the time, in 1996, and 8 of them had died quickly. Hanhart syndrome results in undeveloped organs and undeveloped limbs, so many machines are needed to keep the babies who have it alive and their organs functioning properly. But when I was born, my organs were working at 100%.

Looking back, all I can see is how rare it is for me to be alive. I am so grateful for life. All of us, including you, no matter what, have life to be grateful for. Life is such a rare thing and takes extreme odds to happen. So many sperm died trying to create you, but you made it. This is one very important reason to be grateful.

You can't be grateful and sad or grateful and angry at the same time. It's scientifically impossible. This is why it's so important to start your day off in gratitude. Start a "gratitude journal" right now. Write down 5 things you can be grateful for every single morning.

You can be grateful for big things or small things. As you get into the rhythm of doing this practice, you will notice more and more things to be grateful for, like the future you want to experience. You can even be grateful for hardships and tragedy because these things help define who you are and what you stand for. Starting every day with gratitude gives you the right mindset and energy to carry into your day, and it will help you erase negative thoughts.

Questions to Answer Before You Continue Reading...

- Who is someone in your life you are grateful for and why?
- What challenge are you grateful for that, looking back, shaped you?
- What are you most grateful for about your future?

_____

_____

_____

_____

_____

_____

_____

_____

_____

_____

_____

_____

_____

_____

_____

_____

_____

_____

_____

"Gratitude unlocks the fullness of life. It turns what we have into enough, and more. It turns denial into acceptance, chaos to order, confusion to clarity. It can turn a meal into a feast, a house into a home, a stranger into a friend. "

Melody Beattie

Chapter 3

How Can I?

"Quality questions create a quality life. Successful people ask better questions, and as a result, they get better answers"

Tony Robbins

My parents understood immediately that my condition was not something they could control. When they received the news of my diagnosis, and that I was going to be born without my legs and without an arm, they handled it extremely well. I look up to my parents as examples of how to live because of the way they handled the situation.

It was extremely hard for them, but they realized, "Okay, this is life. We can't control this, so we just need to see where it goes." We just need to focus on the positive.

I was born on May 20th, 1996. As soon as I came out of the womb, the doctors handed my parents a list of all the things I couldn't do. They said, "Your son will never be able to feed himself. Your son will never be able to adjust himself in a chair. Your son will never be able to walk," etc. The list went on and on. Basically, they told my parents, "Your son will be a big baby for the rest of his life."

My parents made a choice right then. We all have to make a choice. We can either let **outside noise** and other people in the world dictate what can and cannot be accomplished, put limits on us and say what we're capable of doing. Or we can choose to find out what we're truly capable of on our own.

My parents responded to the doctors by saying, more or less, "We're not going to give up on what's for possible for our son that quickly." They didn't care about the limits that were being put on me. They just wanted to wait and see how I could progress with my life.

Not everyone is born with doctors telling them they aren't going to be able to do normal, everyday tasks, but many people are focused on what others think about them and their capabilities. They believe in the limits that other people put on them. If you think this way, what you need to realize is that **the only limits you have are the ones you put on yourself.**

We all define what we are capable of doing, whether we are conscious of it or not. My parents had to make the decision to tell the doctors, "We're going to wait and see what happens." They were not in denial. They accepted that my life was going to be a challenge, but the outside noise did not influence their approach to the situation.

For you, the outside noise you may have to contend with might be close family, close friends, or anyone who tells you, "You're not good enough. Your goals are too big. What's your plan B?" Ignore these people!

On the flip side, it's great to have people supporting you and listening to you when you talk about your plans, but guess what? The only person that truly needs your support is yourself. No one else can run the vision you have for your life to completion. That's your job.

All those people out there talking about you, whether positively or negatively, you can't control them. This is why it's important to stop worrying about people's opinions and to stop worrying about situations you have no power over, and to start focusing on things you do have power over.

My parents sat me down at an early age and told me, "Nick, the world is not going to stop for you because you were born like this. You're going to have to figure out how to do everything Nick's way." They made it clear to me that some situations in life were going to be hard for me.

For example, they sat me down in the most polite way they could, put my clothes in front of me, and said, "Alright, Nick, figure out how to put your clothes on by yourself." They also sat me down in my high chair, put food in front of me and said, "Alright, Nick, figure out how to eat on your own, because mom and dad are not going to be around all the time."

Many parents do everything for their kids. They don't let their kids "fall on their face." They put them in a huge bubble. I'm so grateful that my parents let me "fall on my face." My parents put challenges in front of me, and because of this I got into the mindset and rhythm of never saying I couldn't do something, but always reminding myself, "It's not can't… It's how?"

They made it very clear to me that I was never allowed to believe that I couldn't do something. They made it clear that everything was going to be harder for me, but that I could, if I wanted to bad enough, figure out how to do everything my own way.

This lesson my parents taught me applies to every single person alive today. You may get flustered when you're challenged. You may face obstacles no one else faces in business, relationships, whatever it may be. But if you take a deep breath and realize that it's never "can't" and always "how can I?" then you will find a way.

When I was a kid, after being challenged many times, I finally realized I didn't need to use utensils to eat Cheerios. If I licked my finger and picked them up that way, I could eat them a lot faster. Every time I overcame a challenge like this, my mind got a little more creative. I also became more driven with each success I had.

I always told myself, "Okay, I need to do this. How can I approach it differently to get it done?" This was my attitude when I was growing up, and it's still my attitude today. I would have been slapped in the face by reality at age 18 if I hadn't been trained to think this way.

The first time I ever rode a skateboard, I did it on my stomach. It was fun this way, but I wanted more. I wanted to go faster. Finally, I realized that if I sat upright on my butt, I could get much more momentum and go much faster.

After I mastered riding the skateboard this way, I learned a new trick. I was excited to show my parents what I had learned to do, so I called them outside to come watch me. When they came out, I took them to a hill nearby and left them at the bottom of it. Then I went up the hill with my board, and prepared myself for what I was about to do.

I pushed off hard, and I went flying down the hill. As I got closer to my parents, I popped into a handstand. My face was two inches from the pavement. My mom was terrified, but I was ecstatic because I had progressed from moving about slowly on a skateboard on my stomach to doing an awesome trick nobody saw coming.

It took me a long time to learn how to do a handstand on my skateboard. Nobody saw how many times I fell on my face trying to do it. They just saw the end result. This is true for so many areas of our lives. We look up to entrepreneurs, athletes, actors and musicians for the incredible things they can do, but what we don't often recognize is how many times they failed in order to become great at what they do.

We don't see how many times people rejected them. We don't see how many times their business plans failed. We don't see how many times people told them that what they wanted to do was unrealistic. We don't see what they had to overcome to become known for being the best at what they do.

If you're reading this book right now, I am going to assume you are on a journey to improve your life. You might not know where you're headed yet, or you might know exactly what you want already. Either way, you're on a journey, so embrace it. Embrace the hard times. Embrace the times where you fail, because that's how you're going to grow as a person. That's how you're going to evolve as a human being.

The journey of life is about picking yourself up when you fall and trying again and again and again. You can focus on all the situations you can't control. You can get angry about all the challenges you face, and you can decide that life is not fair and that you should just give up trying. But that kind of thinking is pointless. It won't get you anywhere.

To grow, you have to realize that you can't erase the challenges in your life. You will never rid yourself of them. You can't even control what they're going to be or when they're going to land right on your doorstep. But you can focus on what you can control and how you react when you are faced with a challenge. You can focus on crushing your obstacles into the dirt, and evolving into a human being that always finds a way to get things done. **The truth is that our problems become gifts once we learn from them.**

Chapter Summary

My parents immediately understood that my condition was not something they could control. As soon as I was born, doctors gave them a list of all the things I wasn't going to be able to do, and basically told them that I was going to be a big baby for the rest of my life. They rejected this idea, and decided instead to teach me how to overcome challenges in my own way.

They put my clothes in front of me, and they told me to figure out how to put them on. They put food in front of me, and they told me to figure out how to eat it. They wanted to me to overcome challenges and learn how to be independent. If they hadn't encouraged me to figure out how to do things on my own, reality would have slapped me in the face when I turned 18.

When I was young, I learned how to ride a skateboard on my stomach. But I wanted more, so I figured out if I rode it sitting on my butt, then I could go even faster. The next thing I learned was how to do a handstand on the board. I shocked my parents by showing them this trick. What no one saw was how many times I fell on my face trying to learn how to do it.

Everyone wants to progress in life. Everyone wants to keep growing, evolving and doing bigger and better things. This is one way we get enjoyment out of life. If we don't evolve this way, we die. Every person that does anything great in life faces tons of challenges, tons of rejections, and many failures before they finally reach their goal. But by focusing on what they can control instead of what they can't, they move forward until they eventually reach their goal.

You can overcome challenges by focusing on you. Ignore the outside noise. Focus on what you can change. Focus on what you can do better. Focus on how you can improve. You will always face challenges, no matter how much you progress. They will never go away. So, never say you "can't" do something. Always ask yourself, "How can I?"

Questions to Answer Before You Continue Reading...

- What is your most important goal right now?
- In what ways are you supported in achieving this goal? For example, what resources, relationships, personal strengths, or skill setsdo you have at your disposal?
- What are 3 of your biggest motivations to accomplish this goal? These are the ideas that give you sense of commitment and determination.
- What are the painful consequences of not accomplishing this goal? What is the MOST painful consequence? (Circle it)
- Why are you committed to accomplishing this goal?

_____

_____

_____

_____

_____

_____

_____

_____

_____

_____

_____

_____

_____

"If you find a path with no obstacles, it probably doesn't lead anywhere."

Frank A. Clark

Chapter 4

Do It For You

"A quitter never wins, and a winner never quits"
Ted Turner

Before I went to middle school, I saw myself as just a regular kid. I didn't realize that I was "different," at least not in any way that mattered to me. The only thing I was somewhat bothered by was my hand. I didn't like the way it looked.

Looking back on old family photos, one sticks out to me the most. It's a picture of my family on Christmas, and I have my hand hidden in my hat. I didn't want it in the picture. I was a little bit self-conscious of it.

As a kid, I was lucky to be in a great school system. I also had great friends. I wasn't bullied very often, which I'm thankful for. There is just one story from my school years that sticks out to me today.

I was in elementary school playing kickball. When I played kickball, the teachers kicked for me, and I ran the bases. At this particular at bat, I ran around the bases, and I slid into home and scored.

I was feeling great about this until one kid looked at the catcher who had been guarding home plate and said, "You're really going to let a cripple score on you?" This made me upset. I started crying immediately.

I wanted to scream, "Yeah, a cripple did beat you, and he's going to beat you over and over again because you suck." I was pissed. This was the kind of stuff I kept in the back of my head all the time. I had a list of all the names people called me in my mind, and I let it torture me often. I hated being called "crippled" or anything like that.

Even after this experience, I still didn't really realize I was much different until I got to middle school. Middle school is usually when clicks start to form, and it's when kids start to become very judgmental. High school and middle school seems to be the most judgmental part of our entire lives. I think it's because we all start to become aware of our shortcomings, and the way some kids deal with that is by putting other kids down.

For me, I started to realize that everybody was taller than me. It started to bother me that I had no legs. I also had an aid in school that helped me get around, and although I wasn't any slower mentally, kids assumed I was because of the aid sitting with me. I was self-conscious about having any kind of help.

I wanted to show kids that I was normal and just like them, but I began to notice that they looked at me differently.

There was some name-calling but usually not to my face. I just overheard what people said, and I noticed the pointing, the stares and the covering of mouths to talk about me.

All of this led to me experiencing my lowest point in life. I became very depressed and extremely uncomfortable in my body. I didn't like being in my own skin. I didn't want to look in the mirror at myself. I was absolutely disgusted with myself. It got to the point where I didn't even want to go out in public because I just thought people were going to judge me.

I didn't feel like I fit in anywhere. I felt like an outsider everywhere I went. All my focus was on the things I could not do. I didn't realize I had zero confidence in myself whatsoever. For a long time, I thought confidence was something you were either born with, or you just didn't have it. I told myself all the time, "I don't have confidence, and I never will."

It got to the point that I didn't even want to live in my body anymore and I started having suicidal thoughts. As I grew closer to high school age, I saw other kids get girlfriends, but girls only liked me in a friendly way. They didn't want to date me and I believed I was unattractive because of the way I was born. I thought nobody would ever see me as an attractive person.

Suicidal thoughts kept coming, but I didn't follow through on them. I realized that if I did, I would cause my family a lot of pain. I was viewed as a positive person, even when I was at this low point. I always had a mask on because

I knew, even as a young kid, that if I came home from school and smiled and acted happy, this was better for my family to see than to see how depressed I really was.

I knew people were looking to me for good vibes, but I didn't always feel good myself. Even at school, people expected me to be positive, so that's how I acted, even though I was hurting on the inside. I felt like this was my role to play. My entire life, people told me things like, "You're such an inspiration. You're such a positive role model for people." Because of that, I did not want to talk about my sadness. I knew that I wasn't happy, but I also knew that I was not a quitter.

I never quit when my parents put challenges in front of me, so how could I allow myself to quit my life? I couldn't. I had to start searching for a way out of the hole I was in. I had to fight against that part of me that was always tearing myself down. I had to build confidence in myself.

We all experience low points in life. You cannot quit in those low points, even when you feel desperately alone. Regardless of what life has given you to work with, it is your duty to use what you have to live to the best of your ability. No one else can do that for you. Your life is a gift. There is so much in this world for you to experience, that you, specifically, were designed to experience.

If you're in a hole right now, the only person that can dig you out is you. The only person that can make a true, drastic change to your life, whether that's in the area of your finances, your spirituality, your relationships or something else entirely, is you. I'm not saying this to come down hard on you. I'm saying this because you must rely on yourself to be your biggest cheerleader. Do it for you. No matter what you have believed up to this point, you are worth it.

Chapter Summary

Before I got to middle school, I saw myself as a regular kid. I did not feel like I was different, except looking back I can remember that I was ashamed of the way my hand looked. I didn't like it. I hid it in pictures. In elementary school, one tough experience stands out to me the most. I was playing kickball at school, and I ran around the bases and scored. One of the kids looked at the catcher I'd scored against and said, "How could you let a cripple score on you?" I stored comments like this in the back of my mind, and I let them torture me.

In middle school, I started to notice people pointing at me and talking about me behind my back. I felt bad about myself because I had an aid in school, even though I was fine mentally. I began to notice that I was shorter than everyone, and that I had no legs.

When I went to high school, I really hit my lowest point. People started getting girlfriends, but girls weren't interested in me. I believed they wouldn't find me attractive because of how I looked, and I had no confidence in myself at all because I focused only on what I couldn't do. I started having suicidal thoughts andI worked hard to put on a happy face at all times. Everyone, including family, expected me to be a pillar of positivity. People were always telling me how inspiring I was, and I did not want to let them down.

Through all this, I came to the realization that I was not a quitter. I did not quit when facing the challenges my parents put in front of me as a kid, and I decided there was no way I was going to allow myself to quit my life. I chose to try to rise above my negative thoughts and live the life I was given to the best of my ability.

We all go through low points in life. Yours may have occurred in the past, it may be occurring right now, or it may be to come in the future. Your gift is your life. No one else can live it for you and it's your duty to make it the best-lived life that you can. The only one who can change it and make it better is you. Become your own biggest cheerleader, and live your life to the best of your ability. You are worth it. Do it for you.

Questions to Answer Before You Continue Reading...

- Think about one of the most challenging times in your life, that at the time, seemed like it was the worst thing that could have ever happened to you.

- Now that this time has passed, look back and ask yourself this question: what did you learn from it? What gift, moment, skill set, mindset or relationship came from it? Examples: resilience, persistence, determination.

- What is something that you are facing right now? What is it that you can learn from it?

_____

_____

_____

_____

_____

_____

_____

_____

_____

_____

_____

_____

_____

_____

"A smooth sea never made a skillful sailor."

Franklin D. Roosevelt

Chapter 5

Can We Cut My Arm Off?

"You will come to know that what appears today to be a sacrifice will prove instead to be the greatest investment you will ever make."

Gordon B. Hinckley

My freshman year of high school, my best friend, Dan Buhagiar, decided to stop wrestling, and he joined the bowling team instead. He had wrestled the majority of his life up to that point, but he decided he wanted to try something new. One day when we were hanging out like usual, he told me, "Nick, you should try out for the bowling team. It'll be fun. All you have to do is throw the ball down the lane, and you get to eat cheese fries."

As an Italian with a big appetite, anything involving food, I was down for. In all seriousness, I agreed because I was looking for something to do. I was looking for a team to join. I was looking for some sort of support system. I wanted to be a part of something. I wanted a bigger group of friends, so I tried out for the bowling team.

I joined the team late, so I got one of their older, outdated uniforms. It was extra-large, and it was kind of disgusting. It sort of made me feel like I wasn't fully part of the team, but none-the-less, I was a part of the JV team.

The JV team was not made up of the best bowlers. The varsity team, which my friend Dan was on, had the starting lineup. Dan supported me, even though evidence was pointing to the fact that I was not a great bowler. He was always saying, "Dude, the JV team is undefeated. Being on the JV team is not a bad thing." Other people did not see it that way. They way they looked at it, sure, the JV team was undefeated—against other JV teams.

All this was soon not to matter anyways, because when I joined the JV team, I gave them their first loss. I know they were kind of pissed off at me because of the loss, but they never said anything to me about it specifically. Either way, I soon realized that bowling was not for me.

I finished up the season that freshman year, and I never bowled on a team again. Dan did the same. Instead of bowling sophomore year, he went back to wrestling. All of my other friends were stud wrestlers, too. My older brother had been a wrestler when he was in high school as well. I went to his matches as a kid.

I always looked up to my brother and all the other wrestlers I knew. They were true bad asses in my eyes. I knew how tough wrestling was, both physically and mentally. It takes a warrior to get out on the wrestling mat. When Dan went back to wrestling, he and all my other friends who were wrestlers started saying to me, "Nick, you always tell people to try new things. Why don't you try wrestling?"

My response to them was, "I can't. My arm." My right arm was about five inches longer than it is now, and my bone was growing faster than my skin. This made the skin super tight around the bone, and it was very sensitive. I couldn't touch it on anything or it hurt. If I wrestled, my bone could literally break right through my skin and create a bloody mess on the mat.

I was not in any shape to wrestle and I was kind of chubby. As I thought more about it, I came to the realization that if I was a part of the wrestling team, I could be with my friends, and it would probably also help me instill more confidence in myself and help me become more comfortable in my own skin.

So, I made a conscious decision to go into wrestling to help me with my confidence. I wanted to shovel my way out of the hole I was in. After I had made up my mind that this is what I wanted to do, I went home to my parents and told them, "I want to be a wrestler."

My mom responded, "Oh, God, no. Wrestling is the most physical sport. God forbid you hit your arm and your bone pops through your skin. Then what would we do?"

It took me all of five seconds to come up with a solution. Without hesitation, I asked my parents, "Can we cut my arm off?" My arm was the only thing holding me back. It wasn't serving me in any way. I really wasn't a very persuasive speaker back then, but I got the point across to my parents clearly enough. A few hours later, we called and scheduled an appointment for my arm to be amputated.

A few weeks later, I went in for the surgery. I don't even remember being taken into the operating room. They put me under, and when I woke up, they had lasered five inches off of my arm bone and made the point around it cushiony so I could literally push with it and not worry about the bone breaking through.

I remember thinking, as I was on the way to have this done, that it was going to really improve my life. Other people might have thought it was strange that I was willing to go through all of this just to be able to wrestle, **but I knew what I wanted, and I was willing to sacrifice for it.**

I walked away from the surgery with 17 stitches in my arm. It felt like my arm was still there, but it wasn't. It was one of the weirdest things I've ever felt. The stitches made it feel like my arm was being pulled off because of how tight they were. When I went back to school, I was the happiest kid that had just cut his arm off. To me, it was worth it. When I wanted to become a wrestler, the only challenge, the only bump in the road, was my arm pain and risk of injury, not the rest of my "disabilities," because I knew that hard work and dedication would simply make up for my lack of limbs.

If there is something you want to do in life, I can guarantee you that there are going to be obstacles in your way when you try to pursue it. You're going to have to make many sacrifices throughout your journey. **If you don't have to make a sacrifice to pursue your dream, then you aren't dreaming big enough!**

Sacrifice is what will propel you towards what you want. Everything worth doing in life comes at a cost. That's what makes it worth doing. If things are just handed to you, then they have no value. If you want something bad enough, give everything you've got in order to achieve it.

Chapter Summary

My freshman year of high school, my best friend, Dan Buhagiar, talked me into joining the bowling team. I joined the JV team, and I quickly realized that it wasn't for me. After giving the JV team their first lost, I finished out the season, and I moved on.

Dan and all my buddies were wrestlers. My brother had also been a wrestler when he was in high school, and I thought all wrestlers were total bad asses. I wanted to join their ranks and be able to tell people that I was a wrestler. I wanted to start digging myself out of the hole I was in, and I thought joining the wrestling team would be the perfect way to do that, but my problem was that my arm bone could pop through my skin at any moment if I was wrestling.

However, I wanted to wrestle more than anything, so I convinced my parents to let me get my arm cut off. I was extremely confident this was the best thing for me to do because it would allow me to join the wrestling team. After my arm was amputated, I was the happiest kid that had just got his arm cut off. The sacrifice was worth it.

Many people are afraid to sacrifice. They're afraid to give up anything, even if it does not serve them. They don't want to give up the things they are used to, even to do something amazing they dream of doing. You have to sacrifice in life to propel yourself towards better things. If something is handed to you, it has no value. If you want something bad enough, you have to be willing to sacrifice everything for it.

Questions to Answer Before You Continue Reading...

- What am I willing to sacrifice now in order to grow in the following areas of my life? Divide into sections: mentally, relationally, physically, financially, spiritually.
- Example: Watch less TV and read more.
- Example: Eat healthy food 5 days out of the 7 instead of eating junk food most of the week.

_____

_____

_____

_____

_____

_____

_____

_____

_____

_____

_____

_____

_____

_____

_____

_____

_____

_____

"If you are willing to do only what's easy, life will be hard. But if you're willing to do what's hard, life will be easy"

T. Harv Eker

Chapter 6

Confidence is Self-Integrity

"Confidence is not "They will like me". Confidence is "I'll be fine if they don't"

Unknown

You can gain confidence in your life by gaining self-integrity. Self-integrity is keeping your word to yourself. If you do not have confidence, it means you have a bad relationship with yourself. It means you're saying you're going to do something, and then you do not follow through.

You can gain confidence in yourself by doing little things. You tell yourself you're going to wake up 30 minutes earlier every day, and then you actually do it. You tell yourself you're going to eat healthy 5 of 7 days a week, and then you actually do it. When you keep your word on the small, little things, mentally applaud yourself. As you continuously keep your word to yourself, you build a better relationship with yourself. You start to know who you are, and you start to know that when you say you're going to do something, it's going to get done.

That is what having confidence in yourself means. When you have a good relationship with yourself, you do not care what anyone else thinks about you because you know who you are. You know your work ethic. You know you have integrity. You are, in a word, confident.

When I told myself, "Okay, I'm going to amputate my arm, so then I can wrestle," that meant I had to hold myself accountable to follow through. When I came out of surgery, I had to move on to rehabilitation. There was more work that had to be done for me to be able to do what I said I was going to do. I built confidence in myself every step of the way.

In middle school, I had a gym teacher named Christopher Loveland who also taught gym in high school and coached wrestling. We're still friends to this day. He used to always ask me constantly, "When are you going to start wrestling? When are you going to get on the mat, Nick?"

People were always asking me when I was going to wrestle, and it was something I wanted to do, but my arm was an obstacle. After I had taken care of that problem, my confidence soared. I realized I was about to do something that really meant a lot to me. Also, I had told people that I was going to cut my arm off and wrestle, and that's what I did.

When I got back to school, people did not necessarily understand why I'd chosen to cut my arm off. They did not understand how I was going to wrestle when I had no legs and one arm. It was the same exhausted opinions I had come up against many times since birth—people telling me I could not do something.

I did not let them deter me. I told people, "You're right. I'm not going to become a wrestler. I'm going to become a varsity wrestler." I had a chip on my shoulder. I wanted to prove people wrong. A year after my surgery, I tried out for the wrestling team, and I was placed on the JV team. It wasn't varsity like I wanted, but I was still determined to work hard.

Most of the guys on the team were my friends, so when I went into the wrestling room, I told everybody, "Look, you guys need to beat me up. You need to go against me as hard as you can. Slam my face into the mat as many times as you need to. I'm not going to become the best possible wrestler I can be if you hold back on me." I told them this because I learned early on that failure was my best friend.

When I was 13 years old, I was on the *Today Show*, and I told Ann Curry on national television, "Failure is your best friend. You learn by falling on your face. You learn by trying and then adapting. If you don't try, you will never know what you can do."

I did not want to be given any opportunity not to fail when I was wrestling. When I beat somebody, I wanted to beat them—legit. I did not want people to hold back on me. I wanted to make kids cry. I wanted to do what wrestlers do. I wanted to pick people up and slam them down. I wanted to push myself further than I ever had, both physically and mentally.

Junior year, wrestling was a huge learning experience for me about how far I could push myself. Practices were brutal. In my senior year, I worked even harder. I got beat up every day. As a team, we got our asses kicked by the coaches sometimes. I knew if I was able to crack a smile even when we were all in pain, I could motivate my teammates to become better and better athletes. I worked on my attitude harder than I ever had before.

I was close with everybody on the team, including my coach, Mike Bischoff. The main guys who supported me the most as a wrestler were Josh Foca, Brett Lyons, Jake and Jeff Paton, Dan Buhagiar, and Nacho Carrillo. They were my main support system. They helped me get through wrestling and also contributed to making me into the man I am today. If any of you guys are reading this right now, thank you.

I knew I was not the best wrestler and that did not hold me back from supporting my teammates on the sidelines. I was always screaming for my boys. I was very vocal. This is when I started to realize, just a little bit, how good I was at motivating people. I realized my energy was very contagious, and I recognized how much I truly care about other people.

Every time I went into the wrestling room, I worked hard to figure out ways I could become a better wrestler.

Everything I learned, I learned through trial and error. Mastering everything in life works this way. So, start small. Try something. **Prove to yourself that when you say you're going to do something, you follow through with it.** This is how you build self-integrity, and self-integrity is confidence. You never know what could be done if you do not try.

Chapter Summary

Confidence is self-integrity. Self-integrity is telling yourself that you're going to do something, and then you do it. To build self-integrity, start by doing something small. This could be anything, like telling yourself you're going to get up 30 minutes earlier every day, and then doing it. This could be saying you're going to eat healthy 5 out of 7 days a week, and then doing it. When you keep your word to yourself, you build confidence.

For example, I said I was going to become a wrestler, and I did it. I made the sacrifices necessary in order to make it happen, and I gained confidence in myself as a result. I did not become the best wrestler on the team, but every day I got better because I wasn't afraid of failure. I also learned that I love motivating people.

Failure is your best friend. All of life is trial and error. When you try and fail, you can course correct and figure out how to do things better. This is how you learn. You never know what you could accomplish if you don't ever try. Start small, build your confidence, and always push yourself.

Questions to Answer Before You Continue Reading...

- What promises and micro commitments can you make to yourself today, that you know you will undoubtedly be able to follow through on?
- What is something that you must commit to, that you know will take your life to the next level? Once you identify it, break it down into small steps.
- What do those steps look like?
- Why is it important for you to take those steps?
- NOW GO DO IT!

_____

_____

_____

_____

_____

_____

_____

_____

_____

_____

_____

_____

_____

_____

_____

"Nothing is at last sacred but the integrity of your own mind"

Ralph Waldo Emerson

Chapter 7

My Quantum Moment

"The meaning of life is to find your gift. The purpose of life is to give it away"

Pablo Picasso

Most of the time, deep down, you know what you really want in life. Sometimes, however, close friends and family have a path in their minds that they think would be best for you, and they try to get you to conform to it.

If you do not follow what your heart is really telling you to do, you're not going to grow. This can be a very hard to understand, and it is why all of us need two kinds of people in our lives. We need people in our lives who will support us no matter what, and we need people in our lives who are always pushing us to do more.

One challenge I've taken on recently is creating a training program to help people who want to improve their lives. One of my main focuses for this training program is to show people that I'm not just a dictator that has a lot of good ideas about what other people should do to improve their lives. I'm a guy that actually practices what I preach.

To show this, I've had to do some things on camera that have been a real challenge. In one part of the training, I talk about how it feels to reach 50% of a goal, etc. The best way I could think of to illustrate this concept was to go out and climb a mountain on camera. Keep in mind, I had never climbed a mountain before this, and I climbed for four hours. It was extremely uncomfortable, but I know that willingly doing what's uncomfortable is what leads to maximum personal growth.

Now, one of the major points I wanted to make in climbing a mountain on camera is that when you make it 50% of the way up a mountain or 50% of the way towards a goal, half of the people around you are going to quit. They're not going to want to keep up with you. Either they don't have the endurance, or they don't have the will to keep going.

The other half of the people around you will be the ones telling you, "You're 50% of the way, but you still have another 50% left. Let's go! I know you're capable of more!" Those people who supported you half of the way are still important, but you absolutely can't survive without the people who push you when you yourself want to quit.

When I was at my lowest point in life, my thoughts were centered on questions like, "Why me? Out of billions of people on planet Earth, why did I have to be born like this? Why do I have to go through these challenges?" Getting a support system built up around me in the form of my wrestling team saved my life.

Make no mistake about it, I got my butt kicked by my teammates and my coaches every single day, but they never let me give less than 100% effort. I had to do a lot of different techniques to keep myself from getting pinned on the mat. I tried all kinds of different strategies in practice against my teammates.

Even when I lost a wrestling match, which was basically every time I wrestled, my goal was to give up less points to help my team win. Each and every time I got off the mat, I asked myself what I could do to get better. In my first year, my record was 1 in 20. My second year, I won 2 matches, so not much better, but I learned every time I lost. This is the advantage of losing. You can view losing in a positive way or losing in a negative way. When I lost, with the help of my team, I focused on how I was going to improve.

My senior year, the gymnasium was packed with people who were there to watch me wrestle. I got standing ovations when I lost. This just pissed me off. I thought to myself, "Why are you clapping for me? I just got my butt kicked. You're not supposed to applaud losing."

Then one time I came off the mat and this lady came up to me crying. She said to me, "Nick, I want to thank you.

My daughter never wanted to do a sport. She never wanted to do any kind of extracurricular activity, but when she saw you out there wrestling, you changed her perspective. You motivated her to do something different. Now she wants to try everything she can."

This was what I call my quantum moment. It blew my mind when I realized that I had been on the mat wrestling for myself and trying to boost my own confidence, but in the process, I had changed at least on person's life in a positive way. The thought occurred to me then, "How many perspectives can I change for the better if I focus my energy on helping people?" In that moment, I realized I was put on Earth to be an example for others.

As I moved along in life, I realized that all the things that I thought were disgusting about myself and all the things that I thought were negative about me were my greatest strengths. I firmly believe and often tell people that the most attractive thing you could be is different. The sexiest thing you could be is different. In business and in personal life, everybody is always just trying to fit in. It's not what you to do to fit in with the crowd that makes you attractive. It's what you do to stand out from the crowd that makes you attractive.

Kids and adults alike are always trying to fit in somewhere. Everybody wants to be part of the "in crowd." When you are your authentic self, you will attract your tribe. You will attract the people you need around you that will go not just 50% of the way up the mountain by your side, but 100% of the way.

Chapter Summary

We need people around us to support us where we're at and to support us to keep growing. When putting together my training program, I wanted to make it clear to people that at different levels of reaching a goal, people in your life are going to either keep going with you and push you to move forward, or they're going to fall off due to a lack of endurance or lack of will.

When I started wrestling, I found my support system. I was not the best wrestler, but every day I did what I could to improve and to give up fewer points for the benefit of my team. I got out on the mat to improve myself and build my own confidence, but other people started to take notice. People packed the gym out to watch me wrestle. I hated when they clapped for me when I lost, but after one match, a woman came up to me and told me something that led to what I call my quantum moment.

This woman told me that her daughter had been inspired to try all kinds of sports after watching me wrestle, where before she had no interest in any extracurricular activities at all. When she told me this, I realized what I was put on Earth to do. I realized I was put here to change people's perspectives for the better, and that if I were to focus all of my energy and attention on doing this, I could help a lot of people.

I believe you were put on this Earth to do something great. You need people in your life that will hold you accountable and push you to keep going when you're only halfway up the mountain. The most attractive thing you could be is different. When you commit to being your authentic self, you will attract the right people who will not only push you to climb the mountain, but will climb it with you.

Questions to Answer Before You Continue Reading...

- What do you get the most compliments or praise for?
- Where and how do you naturally shine?
- What makes you come alive?
- What thing do you do that makes time feel like it doesn't exist, where you feel fully present?

_____

_____

_____

_____

_____

_____

_____

_____

_____

_____

_____

_____

_____

_____

_____

_____

_____

_____

"Your mission: Be so busy loving your life that you have no time for hate, regret or fear"

Unknown

Chapter 8

Be Yourself

"They laugh at me because I am different, I laugh at them because they are all the same"

Kurt Cobain

When I was a senior in high school in 2014, the Vine app came out. It blew up immediately. Everyone was on Vine, and I decided I wanted to make videos for Vine, too. Prior to Vine, I posted videos on YouTube, so I knew the internet was going to judge me no matter what I put out there, but my confidence was high.

Wrestling gave me the confidence to put myself on the internet. I literally did not care what anyone thought of me. I posted whatever I wanted. I wanted to put something on Vine that no one had ever seen before, because I knew there was a good chance it could go viral.

I wanted to make something that would hook and make people freak out. One day when my friends and I were hanging out, we talked about what kind of video I should make to put on Vine. I came up with an idea in my head, and then I asked all my friends, "How many legless guys have you seen crawling around Walmart pretending to be a zombie?"

Their response was, of course, "None."

So, I put fake blood on my face and clothes and went to my local Walmart in Lacey, New Jersey (which I'm not allowed in anymore). With my friends with me, we walked through the aisles looking for a victim. Finally, we came upon a man who was heavily invested in picking out the perfect paper towels. He looked so focused that I knew I could catch him by surprise. On the sly, I whispered to my friends, "Record this," then I went around the corner and crawled up on the guy as fast I could and went, "Argh!"

He yelled, and then he threw the paper towels he had finally picked out right in my face. My friends captured all of this in six seconds, and we had what I thought was the perfect Vine. I apologized to the man, and then we left the store.

I told my family and friends that if this video reached 500 people, then I would be happy, since I had experienced what it felt like to be disgusted with my own body. I knew what it felt like to be uncomfortable in my own skin. I knew there are millions of kids and adults who feel disgusted with themselves and believe they aren't good enough every single day. By just putting myself out there online, my goal was to make people say to themselves, "Wow, look how happy Nick is. He's out there messing around and making the best of his situation. Maybe I could be happier in my situation."

I posted this zombie video on Vine hoping it would help somebody have a better day, and then I went to sleep. When I woke up, the craziest thing ever had happened. The video had over 80,000 likes and over 80,000 re-Vines. It went internationally viral. It was at the top of the popular page for days. People were freaking out over it. It was everywhere

When I arrived at school, people kept telling me, "Dude, your Vine is blowing up. You're zombie king." I gained 50,000 followers on Vine over night. There were even news articles about me. In the following days, people contacted me to do interviews left and right, all over the world.

One article that came out that stood out to me the most was titled "NJ Teen, Born with Disability Turned Into a Positive." That was exactly how I wanted my video to be viewed. I wanted people to see that life hands everybody a different deck of cards, and what matters is how you play the game with the cards you've got. I wanted people to see that they should make the best of every situation. I wanted people to think, "Damn, I thought I had things to be insecure about, but what am I complaining about?" I wanted to be a role model in my own unique way, and I wanted to use what is typically seen as bad to bring happiness and good vibes to other people.

What ended up happening was I gained a million followers on Vine in under a year. In that timeframe, I heard every insult in the book in the comments under my videos. I did not let the comments bother me, but I used to get so upset when my parents would read the comments. I had to tell my mom, "Please, stop reading the comments. It's stupid stuff in there. People are calling me some crazy stuff, but I don't care."

Now that I had this platform and outlet, I continuously posted a variety of funny videos to my page. No one had ever viewed anything like what I was posting before. I just wanted to make people laugh and feel good, but my popularity on Vine eventually led to me getting hired by FOX International to scare Norman Reedus from *The Walking Dead* in Tokyo, Japan. Talk about an unexpected turn of events.

I was a senior in high school when FOX reached out to me and hired me. They told me very strictly, "You can't tell anyone about this. You need to keep it secret." It was so hard not to tell people. I was 18 years old, and the price FOX had agreed to pay me for this one prank was enormous. It was extremely hard for me to keep my mouth shut about this because it was just so unreal, but I did. I never told anybody.

Around this time, I started to become known in my school. I became popular because of what I was doing online and I kept the same friends. I kept the same crew. I did not want to hang out with other people just because I now had some notoriety. Weird things started happening, like when I went to another high school to wrestle, and all of their cheerleaders starting cheering for me.

It was cool. I liked the attention. I had fun with it, and it made me feel good, but it didn't change who I was. The whole purpose of making the videos was to help other people feel good. They were not about me. When 50 girls waited outside of Applebee's to meet me while I was eating my food, I did not complain, but I didn't want fame to change who I was.

My number one goal has always been to inspire other people to do what they love without worrying what other people think. It's such an incredible feeling just to give up worrying about always trying to make other people happy. You can never make everybody happy, and you can never make everyone like you, no matter how hard you try. I firmly believe that the best way to live life is to just be yourself.

Recognize that you are already amazing, even if the only people who know you are your family and friends. Fame comes and goes, but who you are as a person lasts forever. Never forget to seek to be the best you can be at everything you do, and always try to inspire others along the way. If you do these things, at the end of your days, you will have lived well.

Chapter Summary

In my senior year of high school, the Vine app was released. I immediately got together with my friends and tried to think of a video that no one had ever seen before to post on Vine. I came up with the idea of dressing up as a legless zombie and scaring people at my local Walmart.

My friends and I made a video of me scaring a man shopping for paper towels, and it immediately blew up on Vine. I gained 50,000 followers overnight, and the video itself got 80,000 views and 80,000 re-Vines. I kept making videos, and in one year, I attracted one million followers.

This led to me getting hired to scare Norman Reedus from *The Walking Dead* in Tokyo, Japan. I was paid an enormous amount to do this, and I had to keep it a secret. Meanwhile, my popularity online was climbing, and people at school started to take notice of me. The reason I started making videos in the first place wasn't to become popular. I made videos to inspire other people.

I wanted to show other people that you don't have to be uncomfortable with who you are. You can be yourself, and you can accept and love yourself no matter what. You are already amazing, even if nobody else knows that. Fame doesn't last forever. If you seek to be the best you can be at everything you do, and you seek to inspire others along the way, at the end of your days, you will have lived well.

Questions to Answer Before You Continue Reading...

- What do you love most about yourself? List these things.
- What do the people closest to you love most about you?

_____

_____

_____

_____

_____

_____

_____

_____

_____

_____

_____

_____

_____

_____

_____

_____

_____

_____

_____

_____

_____

"To be authentic is to be at peace with your imperfections"

Simon Sinek

Chapter 9

Toxic People

"You are the average of the five people you spend the most time with"

Jim Rohn

Some people are toxic. For example, you might have friends who aren't productive. They're stagnant, and they aren't growing. It's not that you should cut these people out of your life. You still have to love them, just not spend so much time with them if you see them going a direction in life that you don't want to go. I have learned it is important to be able to make this distinction about people. It's a big part of knowing your worth.

Are the people you are constantly surrounding yourself with elevating you or sinking you? You need to know your value. You need to know what kind of person you are and what you want to get out of life. Once you know these things, it becomes easy to see what kind of people you should associate with. They say **you are the average of the five people you spend the most time with**. If you want to progress in life, then you have to surround yourself with people who are hungry for progress.

This means surrounding yourself with people who are doing things to make themselves better and trying to move forward. Being stagnant is a bad sign. **You deserve to be great.** You need to know this. You need to have studs in your peer group. You need to have people in your peer group that are just killing it at what they love to do.

If your relationship with someone is one where you are not mutually benefiting each other, you need to step back from it because eventually it is going to sink you. If you surround yourself with the wrong people, they will hold you back and make you do things that you would not do if you were truly acting in your own best interest.

In high school, some of the people that I kept company with and enjoyed and loved were not people who inspired me to be a better person. I saw the good in them, and I loved them for who they were, but that did not mean that every relationship I had was in my best interest. Not everyone I was around was a positive influence.

Let me be clear. I recognize how very hard it can be to move on when you are comfortable with a certain friend group or a certain way of life. When I moved from New Jersey to Florida, it was extremely hard for me to tell my buddies that I was moving, but I knew it was what I had to do to keep seeking new opportunities for growth in my life.

I personally believe that everyone deserves the opportunity to do great things in life. You, reading this book, deserve to be surrounded by great people and connections that will uplift you and help you achieve your goals every single day of your life. Unless you intentionally cultivate these sorts of relationships in your life, they don't happen. A status quo relationship where you just get along with somebody well enough to call them your friend is not good enough. You need to know that the people closest to you are going to be there for you through thick and thin, with your highest good in mind at all times.

In your life, if you have relationships that do nothing but drain you, then you owe it to yourself to reevaluate those relationships. To choose to love someone who from afar is not a selfish choice. It's a choice that ultimately means you are letting go of what doesn't serve you in order to bring the greatest good into the world that's possible. That is far from a selfish act.

What often happens in our social circles is everyone builds habits together. We create unspoken contracts about what is acceptable in our circle. Sometimes, we hurt each other by allowing each other to do things that aren't healthy. Sometimes the problem is less obvious. Sometimes the way one person in a social circle thinks rubs off on everybody else. If one person starts thinking negatively, pretty soon everybody catches on to that. Our friends' thoughts become our thoughts. What we see our closest friends do, we do.

If your friends are always making excuses about why things are the way they are in their lives, you start making the same excuses. Conversely, if your peer group talks optimistically about their goals and their future, you'll start to do that, too. If the people around you are serious about painting a vision of their future and going after it, this will rub off on you.

When your peer group is positive, what you really have is a built-in support system that will help you keep pushing towards better and better things. You want your peer group to be full of people you can bounce ideas back and forth with. You want to surround yourself with people who are reliable, knowledgeable, and have depth and substance.

Now, let me be clear. It's to nobody else's fault or glory if you succeed in life. Ultimately, you have to make the decision to hold yourself accountable. A lazy, uncommitted person who is friends with five different millionaires is never going to make that kind of money for themselves just because they know people who do. Nobody is handed anything in life, even if they seem to have all the right connections. It takes more than connections to create a successful person.

If you have the true desire to succeed, who you surround yourself can definitely help you reach your goals. Knowing who you should surround yourself with requires self-awareness. Don't live in denial and tell yourself that the negative friends you have are the only friends you will ever be able to get. That's a very limiting belief, and it needs to be challenged.

The way you might challenge this belief is by going out into the world and trying to make new friends. This might not happen quickly. In fact, you might even find people who you thought would be good for you, who end up being totally different. That's fine. As I've said over and over in this book, **what matters is that you keep trying**. Every time you try, you learn.

For example, when I decided I wanted to get into bodybuilding, there was no information out there about how a guy with no legs and one arm could start lifting weights. I had no clue what I was doing when I first got in the gym. I didn't know what was going to work, but I kept trying until I figured it out. Now I get messages from other disabled people all the time telling me how much I inspired them to get into the gym and start working out.

I even received a video from a mom of a kid who has no legs. Because of my videos, he was able to figure out how to shimmy back and forth to get around like I do when I do my cardio.

I honestly feel that having inspired a child like me who is growing up with the same challenges I grew up with, I could stop doing what I do now for the rest of my life and feel that

I've already achieved enough. I know there are even more lessons that I have to share.

One of those lessons is the importance of surrounding yourself with the right people. Even if you're in a dark place right now, and you believe that you don't deserve to have great friends around you, I want to tell you that's simply not true. It might take major strength for you to walk away from negative people in your life for fear that if you do that, you will have no one else left.

I'm begging you not to make the mistake of giving up before you try. It will be hard to do this. It will be a sacrifice. I truly believe that if you make a conscious choice to surround yourself with the right people, it will be one of the defining choices of your life.

Chapter Summary

Some people are toxic in life. These are people who don't support you in your goals, or people who are stagnant, not progressing and not growing. If you keep the company of people who are always negative and complaining about their situations, eventually this will rub off on you. You will become someone who is always negative and complaining.

If you stay around people who are positive, talk about their goals and talk about the vision they are painting for their future, then this will become the way you operate as well. We are social creatures, and we adopt the habits of the people that we surround ourselves with. They say you are the average of the five people you spend the most time with. Make no mistake, you are still responsible for yourself and for your decisions, but the people you are around most often can and will influence you.

You may need to make the hard decision to not be around certain people you've grown comfortable with having in your life. This doesn't mean you don't love them. It means you need to love them from afar to be able to live up to your own potential. This isn't a selfish thing to do. We are all here to live out our purpose, and we have to make sacrifices in order to do that. While we may have to spend less time with some people that we still love, when we do this, we're able to impact others in a greater way.

Don't believe the lie that if you cut negative people out of your life, you won't be able to find anyone else to be friends with. It might be hard, but if you intentionally seek out more positive influences, then you will find them and your life will be better for it. Don't give up before you try. This has been a great lesson in my life that I've learned in countless ways, including when I decided I was going to start bodybuilding and lifting weights.

Through trying my hardest to figure out how to do this, and sharing my success with others, I've been able to inspire others with similar disabilities as me to work out and better their lives. One of these people was a little boy who was born without legs and learned to "shimmy" just like I do.

Never give up on anything before you try. It may be hard for you to let go of toxic people. It will be a sacrifice, but if you do your best to fill your life with positive people, it will impact your life in a profound, defining way.

Questions to Answer Before You Continue Reading...

- Who in your circle makes you feel supported and inspired?
- Who should you spend more time with?
- How can you spend more time with people that support and inspire you?

_____

_____

_____

_____

_____

_____

_____

_____

_____

_____

_____

_____

_____

_____

_____

_____

_____

_____

_____

_____

"Your mind is a garden. Your thoughts are the seeds. You can grow flowers. Or you can grow weeds."

Unknown

Chapter 10

Turn Ls into Ws

"We are the architects of our lives and each and everyday we have the ability to learn whatever we want to learn and implement into our lives"

Nick Santonastasso

When you take an L and extract the good, you turn it into a W. If you do this for every loss you experience, life becomes all wins. This is a great way to view everything in life because it allows you to realize that everything that goes wrong can be viewed positively. If you get really good at looking at things in your life this way, your fear of losing will totally disappear. Nelson Mandela once said, "I never lose. I either win or learn."

As I explained earlier in this book, I built my career online through making prank videos and amassing followers on Vine. At the height of my popularity on Vine, things were going very well for me, and I was given the opportunity to move out to LA to film a pilot for a new prank TV show.

At the same time, I had just been accepted into college, and I had even gone to orientation to get all set up to start classes, but in my heart, I knew I didn't really want to go to college. The opportunity to go out to LA to film the pilot for the prank show offered me a salary, and I knew that I would never forgive myself if I turned it down.

So, I moved out to LA after talking through some initial reservations my parents had about the whole situation. I signed a lease for a crappy loft in LA for about $2,000 a month. A week after I signed this lease, I got a call from the show. They told me, "Hey, Nick, just want to let you know, the show didn't get picked. So, thanks, bye." That was it. My show was cancelled, and this also meant I now had no money coming in to pay my bills.

I was now stranded in LA away from family and friends, and I was going broke. It was really hard for me to accept this because one of the big stresses in my life, even growing up and going through middle school and high school, was the fact that I simply couldn't do some jobs that other people could. My number one fear for a lot of my life was how I was going to become financially independent and take care of myself.

When my show was cancelled, life came crashing down on me again. I didn't even have a bed in my apartment. I was sleeping on a pile of towels. This was the first time in my life that I actually went hungry. I needed to pay my rent, so I barely had money for food. I ate tortillas and peanut butter because that's all I had. Things looked hopeless, and I fell into the victim mentality. All I could think to myself was, "Okay, now what?" And I didn't have an answer to that question, so I was stuck in a negative feedback loop where all I could ask myself was, "Why me? Why did this show have to get cut? Why can't I support myself like I wanted to?"

My next move was humiliating. I had to move back home into my parents' house. At least with a place to stay and food to eat, I could begin to plan my next move. I didn't know exactly what that was going to be, but the one thing I could not get out of my head was that I really wanted to work on my fitness.

When I went out to LA, I had in my mind that I was going to get jacked and then come back home and have people think, "My God, he's in such good shape." I didn't know at that time how much work it was to really make a transformation in the gym, but when I came back home not by choice, I decided to take the long view and really dedicate myself to getting into great shape.

I thought that if people could see what I was doing with fitness, it would bring them some value. There were two friends that helped me in the beginning stages—Josh Foca, who I wrestled with, and Ryan Lyons, the older brother of my best friend, Brett Lyons. It took me a long time to figure out what lifts I could do and how I could do them. It was a huge learning experience, and it was a total shift from everything I had done up to that point. I had made a name for myself through pranking, but now my focus was on pushing myself to do something even better and more significant than I had ever done before.

From a business perspective, I thought I might be able to make some money as fitness model. The one thing you can't buy is a fit body. It's also the one thing that nobody can take away from you.

As I started working on this new goal for myself, seemingly out of nowhere, I told the million followers I had on Vine that I was done pranking. My heart just wasn't in it anymore. I wanted to focus my energy on something else, and I told everyone that. I declared that I was going to take over the fitness industry, get into modeling and become a keynote speaker. I had no idea how I was going to do these things, but I was determined to figure it out.

To people on the outside, this probably looked like a crazy, reckless thing to do. I had a million people that loved me for my pranks, but my heart wasn't in it anymore. If there's one thing I know, it's that when your heart is no longer in something, it's time to move on. I had to do what I felt would best support me and my happiness in the long run, and I could not allow myself to continue to do pranks just because that's what everyone expected of me.

I lost big when I went to LA, but I found the W in it. One of the Ws is I learned how it feels to live with absolutely nothing—no money, no bed to sleep in. I learned how to get by with very little, and I gained perspective. I can always be grateful now when I lie on an actual bed and have more food than tortillas and peanut butter.

I regrouped and discovered a new path to pursue that felt much more meaningful. Whether my show got picked or not was completely out of my control. I almost got stuck in the victim mentality, but instead what seemed like a dead end turned out to be the birth of a brand new chapter of my life that has led me to where I am today—and to the creation of this book that you now hold in your hands.

When a door gets slammed in your face, and there's nothing you can do to change that, it hurts. You can recover. You can find a new purpose, one that strikes a deeper core within yourself. There are no dead ends in life. There are only forks in the road. When you lose, find the good in it, learn to play another game if you have to, and you will win again. It's only a matter of time.

Chapter Summary

I built my online following by doing pranks on Vine. As I ended high school and got ready to go into college, I was given the opportunity to go film a pilot for a prank show out in LA. A week after I signed my lease on a $2,000 apartment, the show was cancelled. I was left with a very expensive lease I could not pay for. I didn't know what I was going to do. I had no money. I ate peanut butter and tortilla sandwiches because I had to pay my rent instead of buy food.

The victim mentality started to set in. How I was going to become financially independent had been a concern in my life for a long time. I remember even in high school and middle school I was worried because I knew I couldn't do some of the jobs I saw other people doing.

I was back at square one, living in my parents' home, and the only thing I could think about was working on my fitness. I wanted to get out of pranking because my heart was no longer in it, so I told all of my followers on Vine that I was going to break into the fitness industry, get into modeling and become a keynote speaker. I had no idea how I was going to do this, but setting this intention brought me to where I am today.

When a door gets slammed in your face, you can find a new path. You can find what's really deep inside of you that you know you were born to do. You can turn an L into a W if you keep moving forward. There are no dead ends in life, only forks in the road. When you lose, there is always something good to take from it. The next step is to find a new game, and prepare to win again.

Questions to Answer Before You Continue Reading...

- What is something you've "failed" at recently?
- What did you learn?
- Who do you know that failed at something, but was able to turn it around and turn it into a "W"? This could be someone you know, or someone that you look up to—a family member, a favorite artist, actor or historical figure.

_____

_____

_____

_____

_____

_____

_____

_____

_____

_____

_____

_____

_____

_____

_____

_____

_____

"I can accept failure, everyone fails at something. But I can't accept not trying"

Michael Jordan

Chapter 11

Touch the Dream

"A man without a plan, is always at the mercy of the man with the plan."

Darrell R. Williams

I personally believe that human beings have the power to speak the things they want in their lives into existence. I even have a tattoo on my body that serves as a reminder that this is possible. It's a simple tattoo that says, "3%."

There was a study done at Harvard that found that only 3% of Harvard graduates consistently wrote down their goals and what they wanted in their future. The result was that the people who wrote down their goals ended up being exponentially more successful than their peers who did not do this. I believe this is a sign of how the universe works.

The trick to the game of life is to start speaking about and writing down what you want in your life. When you start telling the universe what you want and working towards it, good things happen seemingly by chance to help you get to your goal. If you are constantly putting good things out into the world, this is true even more so.

I could tell you countless stories of times where I've literally manifested exact things that I wanted, but there is no substitute for you having your own experience with this. If you want to know if this is for real, try it for yourself. Even if you don't believe the universe is capable of this, you still have to know what you want out of life in order to be able to get it.

You need something that pulls you forward. You need a vision. You need something in front of you that you always look at to remind you why you're doing what you're doing. Without something like this, it is very easy to get frustrated when you're working hard and things don't seem to be going your way.

You might be surprised to find that a lot of people don't even know what they want in life. If you take the time to figure this out, you're well ahead of most people. I'm not just talking about material positions, although those might be part of your vision. Focusing on who you actually want to become is just as important as focusing on the things you want to acquire throughout your life.

You have to take the first step and ask, "Okay, who do I want to be? What do I want to do in a year? What do I want to do in two years? How do I want to make money? How do I want to impact people?" From there, when you dedicate yourself to your vision, the universe will place the right people and circumstances in your path to create your highest good.

Just talking about your dreams, thinking about them and sharing them with other people is very powerful. Not long ago, my manager and I were sitting outside together looking at the stars, and he said to me, "Let's have a conversation— you, me and the universe." We talked about all the possibilities for the future, and we stared up into the vastness of space. We both came away from that conversation feeling like we had set into motion some really powerful experiences yet to come in our future.

You don't have to be outside under the stars to let the universe know what you want to experience in your life. You can make your desires known just by writing down your goals like you've already achieved them. For example, one thing I really want to get for myself one day is a Corvette Z06. When I write about this in my journal, I write, "I just bought a Corvette Z06, and I'm so grateful for it."

Writing things down this way or speaking them into existence this way allows your mind to connect with whatever you want to do as already being done. When your energy and focus is concentrated on your vision for your future, opportunities for you to take hold of your vision begin to come into your life. People will literally drop into your life out of nowhere that have connections you need or know how to do something you desperately want to do, but you have to be consistent about focusing on what you want.

One thing you can do to keep yourself accountable to your goals and to continue to always look for opportunities to bring them to life, is get a notebook and write down your goals and desires in the morning. Then, when you go to bed, write them down again. When you do this, be specific about what you want, and believe as if you already have everything you could ever want.

Another way you can start your day off the right way in the morning is by putting on some relaxing music, and then thinking about the first five things that you're grateful for. It's important to not only be grateful for what is to come, but to be grateful for all the amazing things you have already experienced in your life.

When doing this exercise, you might think about, for example, a Christmas you spent with your family when you were 10 years old. Really visualize this in your mind. Look around you. Who was there? What was the atmosphere like? What was so special about this moment? Feel the gratitude bubbling up inside of you when you take time to remember moments like this in detail.

Another exercise you can do is think of a moment when you felt guided in your life, a moment where life just happened for you. It doesn't matter who you are, I bet you've experienced this phenomenon before, but we often don't give these things much thought in our daily lives.

Right now, as I write this book, my team and I are busy scheduling our first speaking tour in China. My goal is to sell out the Beijing National Stadium with 100,000 people in under three years. To keep this goal at the top of my mind, I've made this stadium the background to my phone. Every single day when I wake up, I look at it and remember what I'm trying to achieve. I try to put as much energy as I can into envisioning this stadium filled to capacity. Putting images of what you want into your mind helps you visualize what you want for your future. In addition to putting images of your desired future on your phone, I also recommend creating a vision board to keep your mind from wandering away from thinking about your goals.

With all of these techniques, it's important to keep in mind that some of your goals are not going to reached right away. If you are persistent and vigilant about seizing opportunities when they are presented to you, the time will come when everything you have been envisioning will be within your reach.

In the meantime, while you are waiting, you can still reach out and touch the dream. If there is a certain car you want, go to a dealership and take that car for a test drive. Take notice of how the seats feel and how the steering wheel responds in your hands. Take notice of just how close you really are to making your dream of owning such a car a reality. When you touch the dream like this, let it pull you. Let it motivate you even more. For more in depth examples and lessons please check out my Victorious program at www.booknicksanto.com

Your life is not a sprint. It's a marathon. As Tony Robbins said in his book, *Awaken the Giant Within*, "Most people overestimate what they can accomplish in a year—and underestimate what they can achieve in a decade!" With focus and determination, you can work with the universe over the long-term to manifest the best possible future you can imagine.

Chapter Summary

A study done by Harvard found that only 3% of Harvard graduates wrote down their goals consistently, and it found that those who did write down their goals were exponentially more successful than others. To me, this is evidence that everyone who wants to succeed in life should make what they want known to the universe and to themselves.

You need a vision for your life. You need something that keeps you moving forward. Writing your goals down is a great way to keep your mind focused on what you're trying to achieve. Write down your goals in the past tense, as if you've already achieved them, and feel what it's like to live in that reality. Do this in the morning and at night to keep yourself focused on and aligned with your goals.

Another way you can prime yourself for success is to envision five things you're grateful for every day. These can be big things or small things. It doesn't matter. You can also think of an experience you've already had in your life that was overwhelmingly positive, picture it in detail, and live it again in your mind to bring a sense of peace and gratitude to your day.

To take hold of what you want, always put it before you. Remember the times throughout your life that you felt guided, where life happened for you. Be grateful for what is to come before it has even happened. Reach out and touch the dream. Go test drive the car you have always wanted. Remind yourself just how close you are to everything you could ever want in life. Your life is not a sprint. It's a marathon. Think long-term, and work with focus and determination with the universe to manifest your best possible future.

Questions to Answer Before You Continue Reading...

- Take some time to write down some of the things that would excite you if they happened to you.
- Is it a dream car? A dream home? A dream vacation?
- How will it make you feel when you achieve that dream?
- What can you do this month to touch your dream? Go touch it!

_____

_____

_____

_____

_____

_____

_____

_____

_____

_____

_____

_____

_____

_____

_____

_____

"Dream Big dreams, small dreams have no magic"

Dottie Boreyko

Chapter 12

Your Core Values

"When your values are clear to you, making decisions becomes easier"

Roy E. Disney

If you learn how to use your emotions as a guide, they can lead you to doing what you love in life and to doing what fulfills you. Most people on Earth don't understand how this works. They believe that their emotions are worthless, and that they should never trust their intuition without examining it thoroughly with their logical mind. Then, what happens is, they spend their whole lives in emotional turmoil, working a job they don't enjoy, and when they come home at the end of every day, to survive, they just go through the motions.

Nobody can truly be happy living this way. People in the modern world have lost touch with themselves to such a degree that they don't even know what they value in life anymore. Because they do not know what they value, they do not know how to make decisions in line with their highest good, and instead they default to making safe choices.

Now, I'm not advocating that you follow every emotional impulse that you have. This is a definite recipe for disaster. So, how can you keep yourself in line with your real emotional needs in life without compromising self-discipline and persistence?

What I've come to realize is that in order to live an emotionally fulfilling life, you have to know what your core values are. Once you've laid them out in front of you, you have to examine them in relationship to your everyday actions, and see if you're living by them. You also have to understand that your core values have to serve you in a way that keeps you feeling fresh and ready to serve the world in the way that only you can.

If you don't know your core values, then you will get caught up in the rat race, pursuing surface level things that will always leave you wanting more. If you pursue only fame, you will always crave more significance. If you pursue only money, there will always be someone you know that has more than you. If you pursue sex-appeal, there will always be somebody who is better looking than you. If you're always trying to be the top guy or girl just to beat somebody else out of position, you will always end up feeling like a loser when you inevitably fall to second place or lower.

Going after things in life that just make you look better to other people will never make you happy. This way of life is a bottomless pit. There's no end to the things you can

112

accumulate or accolades you can attach to your name. No matter how much you achieve, you will always want more. This is why it's critically important to know what your core values are and to work towards embodying them in your life. Living your core values is the only way to experience fulfillment in life.

Last year, I was traveling and on my way to a Tony Robbins' event called Date with Destiny. While I was on the road the morning of the first day of the seminar, I got a call from my dad who told me that there was a family crisis. All I could think to myself when I got this call was, "Why? Why did this have to happen right now?"

I didn't know how to help, and the phone calls kept pouring in from everybody in my family. Everybody wanted me to somehow straighten everything out while I was on the road. I just wanted to soak up the knowledge at the event I was going to, and not have to worry about anything else.

I was going through a whirlwind of emotions as Tony got up on stage to speak and open up the event. Oddly enough, the very first thing Tony had us do was break down our core values. What came to my mind was that one of my top values was contributing to and loving my family. In light of this, it kind of started to make sense to me why everybody was calling on me to fix what was going on in my family.

Throughout my life, I had continually put myself in position to be this person for my family, and it is a position I truly find fulfilling to hold. With this realization, my mind started to quiet down, and I continued to process the rest of my core values. What I realized going through them is that in my desire to contribute to other people in my life, I have to include myself as well.

Because I want to be a lantern light for other people when they need help, I have to spend time filling myself up with oil to burn. Yes, it was part of my core values to be there for my family, but what I didn't realize was that I wasn't living my values fully because I also needed to include myself in the persons that I enjoy caring for.

Maybe you can relate to this. If you're a person who is continuously giving to others and acting as the glue for people's relationships, eventually this becomes exhausting. You come to a point where you absolutely must take a break and recharge yourself. When I examined my values, I realized I was in the habit of never taking a break, never taking a vacation and never paying attention to my own needs.

Self-sacrifice can be an admirable quality, but it's not sustainable long-term. Eventually, it becomes a depleting cycle. When you do nothing that's just for you to enjoy, you don't have joy to pass on to others. That isn't the kind of life I want to live, and that's not how I want to treat other people either.

When you look at your core values, they may need restructuring to reflect what is realistic for you to expect of yourself. For example, for a long time, my top core value was definitely contribution. I wanted to give everyone everything that I could give them in order to make their lives better. Like I said earlier, I forgot to include myself in that, but I also lost sight of the other values I have that allow me to contribute to the world and the people close to me in the ways that I want to.

Instead of putting contribution at the top of my list, I determined that I needed to restructure my list of core values. Now they are determination, growth, love, joy and contribution—in that order. Pursuing these things in my life in this order keeps my life balanced. This order of priority serves me best.

Thinking this way isn't selfish. What's selfish is the victim mentality that believes you don't have the power to structure your values and priorities in life. You do have the power to do this. In fact, it's your responsibility to do this, or you won't have a happy life, and you won't be able to help other people in any way, no matter how well intentioned you might be.

Do more things for you. You're not a machine. You need to find time do things that make you feel good. If you don't, you can achieve all the success in the world and still be miserable. Tony Robbins says, "Success without fulfillment is the ultimate failure." There are people whom I have met and hung out with who you might think would be the happiest

115

people in the world because they have everything, but having material success means nothing without fulfillment.

I know people who have millions and millions of dollars, and they are just not fulfilled. Their mind is only focused on what's next. Now they need billions because they believe that will make them happy, but it won't. It can't.

I don't have the money some of the people I've met have, but I still feel that I'm rich. I'm rich in experiences. I get to help people, and I also get to travel and see the world. There's not a lot of money in my pocket, but I feel amazing. That's because every day I do things that make me feel good. I'm constantly working towards living out my core values.

The great thing about all of this is that there is no one size fits all. Your core values are unique to you. They are likely not the same as mine, and that's a good thing. I suggest that you spend some time uncovering what they are, and then finding out what order you need to put them in that will enable you to live them every day. Write down your five core values right now, and paint the picture in your mind of what your life could be like if you lived them every single day from here on out.

Chapter Summary

Your emotions can be a valuable guide in cluing you in to what you love to do in life and what you find most fulfilling. This doesn't mean that you should make rash decisions based on emotion and forget logic. The way to live in touch with your emotions is to live in touch your core values. Living your core values in life is how you experience fulfillment. Surface level achievements will never bring you happiness.

One of my core values has always been loving and contributing to my family. I love helping other people. This includes friends and the people I meet when I'm speaking on a regular basis. Contributing to the betterment of other people's lives brings me joy, but what I let myself forget for a while was that I also need to take time to contribute to myself. If I want to be like a lantern and give light to other people, then I need remember to refill myself with oil to burn.

Last year, when on my way to a Tony Robbins event, my family was going through a crisis and everyone was calling me for help. This was bad timing for me because I just wanted to focus on the event, but one of the first things we did at the event was a deep dive into laying out our core values. I realized then that it was in my core values to be there for my family, but that I needed to prioritize my values in a way that would allow me to do that without burning myself out.

It's important that you put yourself first and structure your core values so they serve you. Every one of us has different values. There is no one size fits all. We all have a responsibility to do what's best for ourselves, and in doing that we are able to do what's best for others. Spend time right now writing down your five core values and think about the order you need to put them in to make sure you are giving yourself the ability to refill the lantern of your life with oil. Then, paint the picture in your mind of what your life would look like if you lived your core values every single day.

Questions to Answer Before You Continue Reading...

- Identify your top 5 core values you are committed to living by. Examples: Intelligence, Health, Determination, Love/Connection, Courage, Passion, Contribution, Abundance, Joy, etc.)

- Think back to a time when you successfully held true to one or more of these values when they were challenged. How did that make you feel?

- What, specifically, are your strengths, unique capabilities and super powers that will enable to you to live your values out loud?

- What would happen if you lived in line with your values, at all times, for the next ten years?

_____

_____

_____

_____

_____

_____

_____

_____

_____

_____

_____

_____

_____

"Your core values are the deeply held beliefs that authentically describe your soul"

John C. Maxwell

Chapter 13

You Are Strong Enough

"Where focus goes, energy flows"
Tony Robbins

Everything life will make you face, you can handle. Think back to a time in your life that was extremely difficult. Maybe you were under a huge financial burden. Maybe a death occurred in your family that was totally unexpected. Maybe you went through a bad break up with a boyfriend, girlfriend or spouse, or maybe a long cherished friendship fell apart without warning. Whatever experience has just come to mind, think back to that critical moment when you thought, "I don't think I can keep going. I don't think I can hang on much longer." If you have that picture in your mind right now, here's what I want you to realize.

You made it.

That time has passed. You made it through. You were strong enough to push through, even when you thought you weren't. You had it in you to keep going, even when it did not seem like you could, the whole time.

I've felt like I could not keep going before, just like you. I've felt like I could not escape what was dragging me down. After going through so many moments of feeling like that, I came to the realization that the only person who could dig me out of such a hole of hopelessness was me.

I'm putting all I've gone through on the line for you in this book, but this is the truth: **you are the only person who has the power to overcome whatever you are struggling with in your life right now**. Realizing this is like finally taking hold of a key that can unlock a locked door in your life. Acting on this knowledge is actually putting the key into the lock and walking through the door to the other side.

Here are some actions you can take to put that key into the lock and start turning. When you're in a low state and you're feeling down, your mind can only think one thought. If it's stuck on a negative one, start thinking about something that has nothing to do with the negative place you keep creating in your mind. Think about something immediate instead. For example, are you sitting or standing? How is your posture? How are you breathing? Are you hot or cold?

When you shift to a state of being self-aware instead of reacting to a negative thought and letting it captivate you, you get some distance from it. When you come to the realization that you're thinking about something negative, change your thinking so it's about something positive. A positive affirmation can counteract a negative one if you determine to take control of your thoughts instead of allowing them to run wild.

On the weekend of my 22nd birthday, I was Miami. What started to get me down was an interaction with a girl that didn't go the way I wanted it to. Because of that, some negative thoughts started to run through my head. I knew these thoughts weren't true, but the experience I had started them in motion. As a result, when I got back home, I was in a very low state. I felt like crap.

Once I realized what was going on, I recognized the need for me to change what I was thinking about. If I didn't make that choice, my mind would have kept creating more and more reasons for me to feel bad about myself. Instead of allowing that pattern to play itself out, I focused on my posture. I focused on my breathing, and then I took a look at what was going on in my head. I found that at the root of it all, I was telling myself I was unattractive, so I changed that. I told myself the opposite. I told myself that I love me for who I am. Once I had reversed the flow of thought this way, more positive thoughts about all kinds of things in my life started to pile up in my mind. Eventually, I was feeling much better.

As human beings, when one bad thing happens to us that makes us think negatively, we start to stack other negative things on top of that in our minds. We build a gigantic garbage heap of negative thoughts. It's hard to live a happy, productive life with a pile of garbage in your mind, so what most people do instead of cleaning up that garbage is they numb themselves so they don't have to notice how big the pile of garbage is that they're living with every day.

People numb themselves to their mental realities all the time. They do this with drugs, alcohol, food, gambling, you name it. The problem with this strategy is that as soon as the "high" wears off, the pile of garbage in the mind has grown even more disgusting and unbearable to live with. It's impossible to get rid of this negative garbage pile by ignoring it. You have to throw it out, piece by piece, positive thought by positive thought.

When you do this consciously, it brings clarity and presence to your mind. This is important for every aspect of life. When you go into a business meeting, for example, you want to be in a good state. You want to be happy, and you want to carry good vibes with you. If you're feeling positive, it's reflected in everything from your posture to your facial expression.

Back when I was in school and was upset, my resting face would just look mad. I didn't realize this until it was pointed out to me, and I started to question how people always knew when I was upset. I didn't realize then how everything that's going on inside of a person is reflected outside as well. This is just one of the many reasons why creating a positive internal state makes such a dramatic difference in your outward life. The things you do and the actions you take in life can also affect your internal state.

Doing good for others can dramatically change your attitude about life. One of the good things I do in the world is work with a non-profit organization called New Beginnings Uganda. With the help of this organization, I was able to give money to a child in Uganda who broke his kneecap from his tibia to his fibula and didn't have money for the surgery he needed. He was going to lose a leg, but with the help of my small donation, his leg was saved. When I feel like crap, I remember this, and all of my negative mind chatter goes away.

Embrace the times when you feel most alive. For me, that's when I'm backstage before I speak and my heart is beating fast and the blood is coursing through my veins. I feel so alive in these moments. Whatever makes you feel this way, do more of that. Then, when life feels unbearable, recall to your mind how you feel when you're at your best. Doing this will give you the strength to push through any challenge. You have already been victorious over so much, and nothing can ever break the spirit of a victor.

Chapter Summary

Everything life throws at you, you can handle. Think back to one of the hardest times you've ever experienced in your life. Maybe it was the death of a loved one, a financial crisis or something else. It doesn't matter what it was, just remember how you felt in those times. Now, realize that you are here in this moment, and that you made it through. You are here today because you were strong enough to get through the challenge life gave to you for your personal growth.

Whatever you are struggling with in life, you are the only person who can overcome it. You hold the key to unlocking the door holding you back from living your life to the fullest. To unlock that door, you have to take action. You have to turn the key.

Don't let negative thoughts make you feel bad about yourself. Negative thoughts tend to pile up like garbage in the mind, and to escape them, many people do things to numb their mind so they don't have to notice the negativity that's inside of it. This is why people turn to addictions, so they can ignore the negative state of their mind.

You have to actively pick apart the garbage pile in your mind for it to go away. When you are overwhelmed by negative thoughts, the first step is to become aware of this.

Then, focus on something immediate like your breathing, your posture or your body temperature. This takes your mind away from the rumination. Next, begin to replace each negative thought with a positive one.

Your internal state affects your external state, and your external state affects your internal state. How you feel affects how other people perceive you, and this affects your experience of life. You want to carry happiness and good vibes with you wherever you go, so taking care of both your external and internal state is important.

Doing good for others can dramatically change your attitude. It can show you that you really are capable of making a difference in the world, no matter who you are. Remembering how you feel when you feel most alive is also a great way to bring immediate gratitude and happiness into your mind. You have already won many battles in life, and the spirit of a victor can never be defeated.

Questions to Answer Before You Continue Reading...

- Think of a recent setback you might have experienced in your work, relationships, health, etc.
- Did you focus on problem or the solution?
- Did you focus on something you couldn't control, or did you focus on something you had control over?
- What was the outcome?
- If it was negative, how could you have handled it differently?

_____

_____

_____

_____

_____

_____

_____

_____

_____

_____

_____

_____

_____

_____

_____

_____

_____

_____

"When you focus on problems, you will have more problems. When you focus on possibilities you will have more opportunities"

Unknown

Chapter 14

Never Sell Your Will to Win

"Life is about taking chances, trying new things, having fun, making mistakes and learning from it."

Unknown

I would much rather live my life with less "what ifs" and more "remember whens." I don't want to be on my deathbed and think, "Man, I wonder if I had done that, what it would have led to?" I don't want to be on my deathbed contemplating all the things I should have done. I want to be thinking about all the things I got to do in life that I loved. You will never know if you enjoy something if you never try it. If you don't try anything, you might miss out on a new hobby, passion or business.

When I moved to Florida in 2017, I promised myself, my family and my supporters that I was going to step on the competitive bodybuilding stage before the year was over. I had no idea what competitive bodybuilding really consisted of. I didn't even think my body was going to be where I really wanted it to be by the end of the year. I decided I was going to get up on the stage no matter what. I wanted to force myself to level up.

To compete, I had to learn how to pose. I had to learn to train the right way to get my body in shape. I had to get the right coach to help me. One of my best friend's, Cody Durakovic, trained me for my entire prep. If you follow me on Instagram, you definitely know who Cody is. If I had waited until I felt fully comfortable and knew everything before I got started, I would have gotten nowhere. Then I would have been left asking myself, "Man, I wonder what would have happened if I had tried that?"

I knew that bodybuilding was going to be hard for me, but that's what I signed up for. Something being hard doesn't mean it's not worthwhile. Doing hard things is what makes life full and interesting. Everything can't be easy. Easy is boring.

I don't know where I would be in life if every time I attempted something and it was hard, I gave up. Everything I've done in my life has been hard. I've had to fall on my face so many times. My life is one big failure that eventually led to success.

I had to learn through trial and error how to do simple things like get on a chair, put my own clothes on and feed myself. After completing these challenges, I eventually built up enough strength and willpower to take on a challenge like becoming a bodybuilder. Building my own confidence up enough for me to be willing to take on a challenge like this didn't happen over night. I had to develop the right mindset over time.

What is that mindset? It's a harder shell. You have to develop a harder shell that will allow you to get knocked around while you're trying to learn how to do something without taking any fatal blows to the chest. You build this shell by shifting your perspective and realizing that the journey is more important than the destination, and that everything is a learning experience.

Right now, drop your ego, and accept that you're going to be bad at basically everything that you try to do for the first time. When this is your mindset, even a small amount of progress you can allow yourself to celebrate. Enjoy the small wins. Let them fuel you to keep trying.

All of us human beings love to see that we're making progress. We love the feeling of moving forward and getting better at things. It's impossible to go from couch potato to world-class athlete over night, but what would happen if you made a commitment to go for a walk two times a week? How could that change you? Would it make you feel a little bit better about your health? Could it inspire you to start eating better and taking your health a little bit more seriously?

The answer is yes. It could, because making small changes over time is how huge changes are made. This doesn't just apply to your physical health. It applies to every area of your life. If you want to be educated, read a couple of pages of a book every day. Read a Wikipedia article about a historical figure who did something great. Neither of these things are huge tasks, but they can and will change the way you look at the world when you do them every day.

If you want to speed up change in some area of your life, create rules for yourself to follow. Create a list of very easy things you can do each day that will contribute to this change, and create a list of things you should simply avoid doing. When you do the easy things that you know contribute to your growth, you have something to feel good about, even if you aren't all the way to your goal yet.

For example, I know I'm growing and changing every time I do a cardio workout or listen to a talented speaker that I can learn from. I also grow and progress every time I lift weights in the gym. I feel good after I do these things because I know they are gradually shaping me into a better person.

I also feel happiness and joy anytime I give someone compliment. I feel good whenever I give a friend a hug. These things aren't difficult to do. They cost no money, and they aren't grand gestures, but they are a way to contribute to someone else's happiness and your own. If you're feeling down, try doing one of these things. You will experience an instant mood lift.

At the end of the day, how you feel about how you spent your day is how you feel about your life. That sounds obvious, but it isn't for most people. Most people don't see how what they choose to do and not do on any given day affects the way they feel about their life as a whole. Doing nothing, remaining stagnant or complacent from day to day, does not lead to happy life.

Always seek new challenges. Always seek new opportunities and situations to push yourself. Action is what kills fear. How committed are you to living a life you love? You might answer this question by saying that you're fully committed, but if you're not actively trying new things, you're committed only in word, but not in deed.

Not long ago, I had the opportunity to be featured on Ed Mylett's podcast. During our interview, he said something that has stuck with me. He said, "There will never be a price for me to sell my will to win." What he meant by this was that nothing, no amount of money or prestige, could ever get in the way of him going after what he wants in life and trying his hardest at every new thing he sets his mind to.

That's the kind of determination all of us need to have. There is no fear in that statement. It means if you will to do something, you are going to do it. It doesn't matter if everybody laughs at you for trying, or even if somebody tries to pay you to quit before you even get started, if you want to do something, do it.

Chapter Summary

I don't want to live my life and look back wonder what could have been. I want to be able to be on my deathbed and remember all the things I did do, and all the things I got to experience that I loved.

You will never know if you like to do something unless you try it. If you don't try something new because it makes you fearful, then you may miss out on making major progress in your life. Human beings thrive on seeing that they are making progress. You make progress by doing things that are new to you and things that help you grow as a person. They don't have to be huge things.

If you want to improve your health, you might try walking a few times a week instead of just sitting on the couch. If you want to improve your knowledge, you might try reading a few pages of a book every day. When you do small things like this, you have something to feel good about, and over time doing small things that change your life in small ways leads to huge life change.

Make rules for your life that are easy for you to follow. Make a list of all the good, easy things you can do to make your life better, and make a list of all the things you should simply avoid doing to make your life better. Throughout the course of a day, if you do one of the easy things, you can feel good because you have made progress. If you avoid doing something you know you shouldn't do, you have made progress. Allow yourself to feel good about this progress, no matter how small.

Fear is defeated by action. Face your fears head on. If you are afraid of doing something, but know it would lead to your growth, do it. You probably won't be good at it the first time, but that's normal. Develop a hard shell so that failure bounces right off of you and you can get back up and keep trying. This is how I've learned how to do everything, even simple things like feeding myself, my whole life.

Most of all, never sell your will to win. Always keep going after what you want. Never give up, even when people laugh at you or try to get you to stop. Always push forward. Always try new things.

Questions to Answer Before You Continue Reading...

- Make a list of all the good, easy things you can do to make your life better. What are they?
- Make a list of all the things you should simply avoid doing to make your life better. What are they?

_____

_____

_____

_____

_____

_____

_____

_____

_____

_____

_____

_____

_____

_____

_____

_____

_____

_____

_____

_____

_____

"If you never try you'll never know."

Unknown

Chapter 15

Be Present

""Realize deeply that the present moment is all you will ever have"
Eckhart Tolle

There's a quote I love by Dale Carnegie that says, "The world is full of people who are grabbing and self-seeking. So the rare individual who unselfishly tries to serve others has an enormous advantage. He has little competition."

Very often, people are not genuine. This can make it hard for the people who are, because many people now live on high alert to protect themselves from scam artists and frauds. There is a silver lining to all of this. If you want to stand out from the crowd and truly succeed, your main focus absolutely has to be helping other people.

In my life, I've now had the incredible opportunity to meet some amazing people, millionaires and billionaires alike. While some people have a view of the rich that they had to have gotten rich by exploiting other people, what I've found is that the opposite is true. People who are truly wealthy are always focused on helping other people. They know that's how value is created in the world, and the people who create value in the world are the ones who are most richly rewarded.

One of the ways I aim to create value in the world is by building relationships with everyone that I get the chance to meet. This is why I always ask to speak at the end of every event I speak at. I want a chance to meet every single person who comes to hear me speak. Sadly, a lot of speakers don't operate this way. They just want to show up, speak, collect their check, and then dip out.

My goal in life and with my business is to be present with people. I want to hear every word they have to say. I don't want to just shake hands while looking around the auditorium in distraction. I want people to know that they matter to me. I want you to know that you matter to me!

It's so important to give yourself fully to other people, to be present with them, and to be present in the world. If you follow the advice I've given you throughout this book, I have no doubt in mind that you will be well equipped to do this. If you're ever feeling lost, just go outside and look up at the sky. Try to really soak in how awesome it is to be alive on this rotating ball of matter that just so happens to be the perfect distance from the sun to be able to support your life on its surface.

You may not understand what your ultimate purpose in life is yet. I believe this is something we all discover as we go. If you can just be still for a moment and remember that just being present in your life and with others is perfect, those kinds of big questions tend to fade away. Life has a funny way of letting you know when you are on the right path when you determine to live this way.

I've had many moments in my life where it has felt like the universe is tapping me on the shoulder and saying, "You're going the right way. Just keep going!" One of these moments for me was when I met The Rock.

I was two weeks out from my first bodybuilding competition, and I decided to go out to Las Vegas for the Mr. Olympia bodybuilding competition to soak up the vibes and inspire myself to stick to the program as my own competition drew closer. Mr. Olympia is a three day event, and on the final day, a Sunday, I decided to hang back at the hotel.

While I was sitting at the hotel, I was feeling inspired by all that I had taken in the previous two days, so I decided I wanted to get a lift in. I headed out to the City Athletic Club, which is a famous gym in Vegas. When I arrived, one of my friends, KC Mitchell, immediately looked at me and said, "Dude, The Rock is upstairs lifting."

Prior to all this happening, I had sent The Rock some videos of me lifting and getting ready for my competition when he had held an online contest for bodybuilders. He had responded positively to my videos, so I knew that he knew who I was already. I didn't want to make a big scene when I heard he was in the gym lifting, because, quite frankly, I was there to pump some iron myself.

Many people in the gym were bombarding him with pictures while he was lifting. I actually kind of felt bad for him, so I decided I was just going to be respectful of his workout time and keep to myself. Five minutes later, a security guard came up to me and asked, "Can Dwayne meet you?" Then he escorted me over to a corner of the gym where I was able to talk to The Rock privately.

Our conversation went something like this. He got down on my level and said, "Bro, I'm such a big fan. I love what you do."

My response was, "I love what YOU do!" Then I told him how much of a role model he was for me, and how I wanted to do what he has done. By that, I meant that I want to break into every industry successfully, from modeling to acting to music to speaking. When I told him this, his response blew my mind.

He said, "People like you and me, Nick, they can put us in any industry, and we will thrive because we know to adapt and overcome new challenges." I will say it again—my mind was blown away by this response. It was a huge confirmation for me that I am on the right path in my life.

Two weeks later, I was backstage getting ready for my bodybuilding competition, and my friend Cody came running up to me and said, "Dude, The Rock just posted a picture of you on his Instagram."

When I looked, I saw the picture we had taken together in the gym in Vegas, and he had also written a message that said, "I want to thank Nick for sharpening my perspective a bit more in life."

This meant so much to me. It confirmed my belief in myself, because if I was able to move The Rock, then I believe I have the power to shake the world. And it's not just me who has this power, it is all of us.

It doesn't matter what circumstances you were born into. Remember, when I was born, my parents were given a list of all things I supposedly wasn't going to be able to do. Today, I can say I've accomplished way more in my life than anybody ever thought was possible, including winning third place in a bodybuilding competition against full-bodied men.

I'm proud of all of the things I've accomplished in my life so far, but most of all I'm proud of the man I've become in the process of pursuing my goals. I could have chosen to be a victim, and nobody would have blamed me. Instead, I chose to be a victor. You have this same choice.

Cultivate a victorious mindset. Never forget that you have the power to do anything that you want with your life. By reading this book through to completion, you have just done something good for yourself that created growth and progress in your life, whether you realized it or not.

Right now, take a moment to stop and just breathe. Be present with your life where you are right now. Focus on what an incredible miracle your life truly is, shift into a perspective of gratitude, and consider this last line a confirmation that you, too, are on the right path.

Chapter Summary

Dale Carnegie said, "The world is full of people who are grabbing and self-seeking. So the rare individual who unselfishly tries to serve others has an enormous advantage. He has little competition." This is why if you want to succeed in life, your main goal should be to help other people. Too many people are not genuine, and this has caused everyone to be on high alert for frauds and scam artists. If your goal is to bring value to other people, you will be rewarded.

Giving yourself fully to other people requires you to be present in your own life. You may not understand your purpose in life at this very moment, but if you keep moving towards it whole heartedly, life will give you many moments of confirmation that you are on the right path.

I experienced one such moment when I met The Rock at a gym in Las Vegas. It wasn't a forced meeting. I had actually decided I wasn't even going to bother him when I saw him in the gym, but the conversation we ended up having and what he posted online after our meeting was a major confirmation that I truly can shake the world.

You, too, have the power to do incredible things in this world. The fact that you have life right now is an incredible miracle. Life is a precious gift, and I truly believe that each of us has a special mission here on Earth. None of us were put here to be a victim. You are here to be a victor! So, never give up. Never stop trying. You have everything you need in order to win at this game. I believe in you, and now it's time for you to believe in you, too!

Questions to Answer Before You Read Another Book

- How can you be more present when you are with your child, spouse or best friend?
- Why is being present important to YOU?
- How will the people you care about feel when they know you are fully present and there for them in the moments when you're together?

_____
_____
_____
_____
_____
_____
_____
_____
_____
_____
_____
_____
_____
_____
_____
_____
_____
_____

"The present moment is the only moment available to us, and it is the door to all moments."

Thich Nhat Hanh

Thank you for reading my book...

I am always grateful to connect with like-minded folks, and find it especially cool to hear from people who have read my books, seen my videos, or attended my speeches. So, if you have any questions or would just like to say hello, go to www.booknicksanto.com and click on the "Contact" tab to send me a message. I look forward to hearing from you, and exploring how I can add as much value to your life as I possibly can!

BOOK NICK TO SPEAK!

Book Nick as your Keynote Speaker and You're Guaranteed to make your event highly enjoyable & unforgettable!

Nick Santonastasso can tailor his message and presentation to suit the needs of your company. Here are just a few examples of the topics Nick speaks on in the corporate sector:

Building confidence
Turning failure into a friend
Persistance
Sound mind, sound body
Living in the state of gratitude
Goal Setting
The power of focus
Annihilate excuses
Leadership
Self Love

Dear Victor,

May I ask you a quick favor? If this book has added value to your life, if you feel like you're better off after reading it, and you see that living with the *Victorious mindset* can be a new beginning for you, I'm hoping you'll do something for someone you love:

Give this book to them. Let them borrow your copy. Ask them to read it. Or better yet, get them their own copy, maybe as a birthday or Christmas gift.

Or it could be for no special occasion at all, other than to say, "Hey, I love and appreciate you, and I want to help you live your best life. Read this". Sometimes a book is all a person needs to get back on track.

If you believe, as I do, that being a great friend or family member is about helping your friends and loved ones to become the best versions of themselves, I encourage you to share this book with them.

Please spread the word.

From the bottom of my hear, thank you so much.

Nick

For more information, please visit

BookNickSanto.com

Made in the USA
Columbia, SC
16 March 2019